COWPOKES WHO CRY

KELCIE MARTIN

ISBN Paperback: 979-8-9875218-2-3
ISBN (ebook): 979-8-9875218-3-0

LCCN: 2023917293

www.cowpokeswhocry.com

Cover Design by Krystal Kramer
Edited by Meg McIntyre at McIntyre Editorial Services LLC
Proofread by Vicki Lee Warner at Vicki's Red Pen
Interior design and formatting by Fox Formatting

To Mom, I get it now.

NOTE TO THE READER

Dear Reader,

    This book contains some stories of miscarriage, birth trauma, and recollections of true events in emergency medical situations. There are also realistic descriptions of animal distress. The emotional moments I write about are very real and raw. I hope that you can all find peace in knowing that although the world we live in is unrelenting, it is also beautiful.

PROLOGUE

SOMETIMES THEY SAY THAT YOUR ENTIRE LIFE FLASHES before your eyes when you die. But what about when you have kids? The look of fear the doctor gave me when I walked into labor and delivery as a "precaution" will forever be branded in my mind. It was the kind of look that felt like, "If one thing goes wrong, all of our lives are at stake." Like everything and nothing I'd done up until that point of my life had mattered. It felt like all the challenges I'd faced before were minuscule. Call me dramatic, but I felt in that very moment that God looked at me, laughed his ass off, and said, "You're one cocky bitch." My entire life I had stood up to any challenge He sent me, but this time I may have met my match.

Maybe that isn't what He was saying, though. Maybe He was saying, "I chose you for a reason." It took a long time for me to come to terms with going into preterm labor. I would feel moments of peace, but the guilt crept back in every once in a while. There wasn't much time in the early days for me to reflect or process those emotions. Between the NICU stay and taking care of premature babies during a pandemic, I was struggling to survive mentally.

After about a year, it seemed as though things started to slow down (as much as they can when you work full-time with two baby boys, who are referred to as Baby A and Baby B in this book to protect my family's privacy). This was the time I was supposed to reflect. This was when I was going to get back to my old self, right?

Wrong.

When I was finally able to breathe again, I felt empty inside. I didn't know who I was anymore; I didn't know who I wanted to be. I found myself rummaging through the get-rich-quick schemes on Google and Pinterest. Maybe money would solve my problems? Who knows what I was thinking, but I was desperate.

This idea kept popping into my head. I continued to push it away.

Maybe I should write a book.

What if I became a famous author?

Remember that creative writing class in college?

The thoughts raced through my head every day at work. I envisioned myself signing books, a best-selling author with popularity and possibly money. I had always wanted to write a book about my childhood. I had always wanted to share my adventures on the ranch where I grew up with the entire world. People wrote books all the time! Why couldn't I?

I was raised in a place my dad considered God's Country, a place where rolling hills and sagebrush were the only things you saw for miles. The horizon looked like the edge of the Earth. Dirt roads interconnected neighbors and small lifelines called towns. The closest Walmart was an hour away. Groceries were bought in bulk and stored with care. Cows bellowed after their babies. Pronghorns pounded the soil beneath their feet. The ground maintained an ecological base, growing the food that started the great circle of life. Humans were scarce, but they were dependable.

Dad worked a tech position in Colorado Springs, Colorado

until Mom found out she was pregnant with me, their eldest daughter. The Western way of life called for my family, and we answered that call with a sense of urgency. When I was three years old, Dad took the ranch manager position at the operation known as Rush Creek Cattle Co. We said goodbye to the resources of the city, and our family moved into the ranch house to begin our life in God's Country.

There, Dad was trusted to manage forty thousand acres of land and everything else that came with it. Just to give you a visual, forty thousand acres is equivalent to sixty-two square miles, about the size of Washington, D.C. Dad and I were cowpokin' these cattle on a ranch close to the size of our nation's capital. Except on this land, no buildings blocked your view, and there were only two homes sheltering three people. The ranch shifted its operations a few times during my stay at Rush Creek. In the beginning, we ran up to a thousand mama cows at once. That means after their babies were born, there were two thousand cows and calves. Over time, my dad realized that the land and water was better equipped to raise young yearling cattle, fatten them up, and sell them. When we ran this operation, there were up to three thousand yearlings stocked at Rush Creek. Over the years, Dad went through a handful of hired hands to help him take care of this vast sea of pasture. But for a lot of the time, I was the only cowpoke he could depend on. The animals outnumbered us, but the experience is something I will never forget.

When Dad told me it was God's Country, I thought he was just saying that because it was pretty to look at. When I had my babies, I was made aware of what God's Country really meant. Everything on that ranch was God's Creation. The animals, the plants, the dirt, the water—those were all God's. But the triumphs, the losses, the lessons, and the strength—those were God's too.

This is where my story began. This is where I decided to find myself again.

CHAPTER ONE

APRIL 2020

"How are you?" my doctor asked, trying to be polite.

The image of the graphic miscarriage I'd had that morning replayed in my mind.

"I've been better," I replied.

I felt numb as the doctor explained that the early loss was a good thing. He said I could try again as soon as I stopped bleeding. The white paint was loud; the walls of the little room made my ears ring. Fluorescent lights amplified the noise as the doctor continued talking. His mouth moved, but there was very little that I could comprehend. I held my stomach, still in pain. It was evident I'd lost weight in the last week. My stomach didn't hang over my pants as I sat on the edge of the exam table. That was the only time in my life I skipped a meal. It was also the only time my heart had ever hurt that badly.

The entire month was hard. I'd hardly told anyone about the pregnancy, let alone the loss. I was confined to my home during the COVID-19 lockdown, teaching science from my couch and wallowing in my grief. Students checked in via email, but my job consisted of posting video assignments and grading little to no work. Not even my career could distract me from the pain I felt.

The hysteria and madness of the virus was a nice addition to my anxiety.

After about a month of wallowing, my good friend Chris invited me on a hike and an outing to Bishop's Castle. The pandemic was in full swing, and I agreed. She knew what I was going through and was trying to get me out of the house.

I felt like canceling the plans, but I threw on my shorts in protest. The world was loud, but the mountains were still quiet.

I stuffed pads in my purse, expecting my period to start. It was a painful realization that I probably wasn't pregnant again. It was also a great relief that my body was OK. Starting a new cycle somehow felt like a new beginning, in some weird spiritual way.

"Sorry, I had to go back for lady products. I think I may start my period today. Crummy." I apologized to my friend as she waited in the driveway to take me on our Memorial Day weekend hike.

"I hope you don't!" she said with an ornery smile.

I know she had good intentions, but the knife stabbed me right in the heart, the feeling of loss still lingering. Her twins, born at twenty-six-weeks gestation, sat in the back seat listening to their mom and I gab. They were teenagers now, and the full, noisy car was warm and inviting. It felt nice to get away from the house and the people saying, "It just wasn't meant to be."

The hike was challenging. The Sangre De Cristo Mountains, although not as large as Pikes Peak, made for beautiful scenery. I noticed my fatigue and blamed it on lying in bed watching *This Is Us* for hours on end. It made me flash back to the angry tears I would cry between episodes. I could see myself sitting in the master bedroom, blackout curtains closed, dried tears crusted on my face.

"Those butterflies keep following you, Kelcie!" my friend's little girl commented. I snapped out of my grief before I got sucked back in. Although she was quiet, I knew she was having fun being a part of the group. Her twin brother trailed a little bit behind us, his goofy comments adding a little comedy to our exploration.

It was strange how the butterflies continued to flock around my face. The monarchs aggressively attacked me, landing on my shoulders. At first it was cute, but it got a little out of hand after a while. My Grammy always told me that butterflies are usually angels of loved ones, following you. I assumed it was the baby I'd lost, and I appreciated that she'd come with me on this hike. It was helping me heal.

We continued on to Bishop's Castle, a very strange landmark in Colorado. A man had the wild idea to build a castle in the mountains, and over time it became a tourist attraction. It was impressive, and also…kind of creepy. The castle was made of stones, and it resembled the shape of a haunted mansion. You know, like something that would be on the front cover of a Halloween movie. The stairs were rickety, and, truthfully, in need of some caution tape, because some places weren't really safe for people to be. I had lived near this location for so long and I had never been. I was determined to climb to the very top. Climb to the top of a tall, rickety, sketchy-looking castle while feeling vulnerable and full of grief. *Nice choice, Kelcie. Nice choice.*

My friend looked at me with a tight-lipped smile. The numb feeling of loss still felt heavy on my chest and my fear was masked. I trudged forward, the twins looking at me in disbelief. I don't think they were as into the idea of tackling the winding stairs as I was.

They became narrower as Chris walked behind me, encouraging me and commenting on every loose board for her trailing children. Her words were there for comfort, but they were somewhat muffled as I continued to move toward the top of the castle. My body felt so tired, but my head felt cleansed by the thin air.

The cool mountain breeze made me stop thinking about why God had taken my first child.

The springtime snow began to fall on Rush Creek, the barometric pressure sending our mama cows into a synchronized labor. Baby calves were hitting the ground at a similar speed to the falling snow. I was only a child, maybe ten years old, but the gift of life was special to me. Calving season was one of my favorites.

"I think she's been here awhile," Dad mumbled as he spotted a cow by herself.

We rolled off of the two-track into the pasture a short ways. The heater was cooking in the cab of the maroon Chevy. Just hours ago, we had a calf defrosting on the floor of the pickup. Dad pushed the clutch in and adjusted the stick as we pulled to a stop. I saw the baby's feet and, by the look on Dad's face, I figured it was another breech calf.

I was familiar with the sound of the calf pullers being scraped and lifted off the back of the pickup. They're quite the contraption. A large metal piece wraps around the cow's behind and connects to a handle. The lever is placed on the long handle between the U-shape that envelops the cow. The chains connected to the lever are eventually chained to the feet of the baby to help them out into the world. We saved many breech babies that way, one crank at a time.

The chains jingled. Something was off, though, and I couldn't quite tell what it was. I got out to observe the situation, staying close to the pickup. The calf pullers wrapped around the mama cow's back end, the chains hooked up to a lever system ready to pull the baby to safety.

He started to pull the lever back...

I waited in anticipation to see the calf's nose, but all I could see was a leg.

Dad cranked the lever once more, and he made a face.

A putrid smell filled the air around us. I immediately ran to the back of the pickup, bracing myself against a back tire as I hurled up my lunch. Our dog proceeded to eat my puke, which made me throw up even more!

"Dad, what happened?" I asked while I covered my nose with my coat sleeve.

"Her baby died inside," my dad answered through gritted teeth. I tried not to speak very much after this because he was in the middle of the smell.

So that's what he meant when he said she had been there awhile...We were too late...

The afternoon sun started to warm the air around us and the aroma intensified. Dad rolled up the sleeves of his plaid button-down shirt; the calf pullers were useless at this point. He began to dig. He continued to put his arm into the cow and maneuver the poor angel baby out of the mama. It was imperative that we get the calf out of her so she didn't die too. The lifeless body hit the ground, and the smell got worse.

Dad took one of our water bottles and rinsed his arms and hands. As we drove away, I watched her. She smelled her lifeless baby, confused and helpless.

"Poor mama," Dad said softly.

Poor mama.

In the days that followed our mountain hike, I continued to wait for my first period to visit me. I was only a few days late, but I knew this could be because of the miscarriage. I remembered the sadness of the cow trying to lick her lifeless baby. In a sense, I related to her, but I also found comfort knowing that I wasn't the only creature on this Earth who had been through this. I wasn't being picked on; it was just part of life.

The schools were shut down indefinitely, and my husband Josh and I found our way out east to God's Country. As long as I had internet access, I could work wherever I wanted. The cattle count was higher than humans and the cornfields separated homes by miles, so it was a perfect way to socially distance.

When we arrived on the plains of eastern Colorado, Mom and I decided to go for a walk. The guys were going out to work cattle, and we had nothing better to do. The spring air decided to be pleasant that day, so we took advantage.

"I think I'm pregnant again, Mom."

"Kelcie, it doesn't happen that fast!" She kind of smiled and then looked at me with concerned eyes.

I think she saw the serious look on my face. There was some-thing about the symptoms I was having—I just knew. Although it had only been four weeks since the miscarriage, it wasn't impossible. The fatigue was hitting me hard, and it wasn't letting up.

The mini mental vacation was nice. The fresh air, the lack of people and news headlines, all of it combined with good food and family conversation, was much needed in my battle with grief. It also distracted me from the idea that I still hadn't gotten my period.

When I arrived home, I took a test to ease my mind.

I still had a few tests left from the last pregnancy, and I cringed when I saw the positive test I'd saved in my toiletry drawer. I set a timer on my phone, waiting the three minutes like it said in the directions. I walked out of the room to keep myself from staring at a plastic stick for three minutes straight. When I walked back in, I felt like throwing up, regardless of the answer. I would be sad if it was negative, and I would be sad and anxious if it was positive. But I knew in my heart what the answer was.

Double lines, dark pink in color. I was pregnant again.

People who have never been through a loss celebrate this moment. Unfortunately, just a few weeks ago, we'd realized we would never have that excitement again. Instead, we felt anxiety and fear. Josh rubbed his bald head with angst. We were both scared shitless.

I was already nauseous, puking immediately upon waking. My uterus almost felt like it was stretching in real time with the growing baby inside of me. It was so different from the first time. What was happening to me?

"I think it's twins," I said as Josh and I showered together. The double shower we added to the new home was my favorite feature, and although most saw it as a sexual thing, it was more of a social thing. For some reason, shower talks always brought out the deep conversations in our marriage.

"I think you're just really anxious. We just need to get to this first appointment." He looked at me in disbelief.

"I know, but I just feel like something is off and it's different this time. I'm hurting, and Mom keeps telling me it's normal, but this just doesn't feel normal to me," I explained as he shaved his beard for work. He was still working as a firefighter and EMT throughout the pandemic, coming in contact with sick patients almost every day. He was in the trenches.

We were in the trenches.

CHAPTER TWO

JUNE 2020

THE AIR WAS HOT, AND MY ANXIETY MADE A NICE BREW IN my stomach to complement my morning puke. With COVID restrictions, we were instructed to wait in the car until they called us into the OB-GYN's office. Luckily, for certain appointments our spouses were allowed in. Any other routine checkup, no one else was allowed in with the pregnant mamas.

"You've had so many symptoms this time. Try not to stress, babe." Josh tried to ease my tension, but the thought of no heartbeat weighed heavily on my brain. The baby we'd lost didn't make it to our first appointment. I was a few days short of my first ultrasound when I miscarried. I ignored Josh without realizing. He watched me as I disassociated. I was also trying to focus on not throwing up.

Thank God the phone rang, because I was wary I would feed the kitties in the parking lot. I pictured my vomit all over the hot, black asphalt, boiling. I walked with haste into the air-conditioned building.

My husband's small talk made me want to throw up all over again! He was trying to calm my nerves, but I could feel his angst as we entered the ultrasound room. He was looking at me, but he wasn't actually seeing me. He was talking to me, but his thoughts were in the past, focusing on the miscarriage a few months ago. He was pretending everything was OK for me, yet deep down, he was feeling the same way I was.

The ultrasound tech looked at me and smiled as she prepared the wand. The room went dark, and we waited for the moment of truth.

It was quiet, and she kept fiddling around with the wand, almost as if she was flipping pages. It reminded me of those toys from my childhood—viewfinders. They were like goggles where you looked inside and used your finger to flip through the different images. They came in McDonald's Happy Meals. *Flip, flip, flip.* The images kept going back and forth. I saw a little gummy bear on the screen, but she wasn't saying anything. The pit of my stomach became a black hole, and I was afraid of the next words.

Please don't say no heartbeat. Please don't say no heartbeat.

"Two babies!" She wasn't flipping screens, she was moving from one baby to the other.

"I FUCKING KNEW IT!" I don't think my spouse and the ultrasound tech were expecting that reaction, but I wanted to point my finger in the face of every person who'd told me I was crazy.

"Kelcie!" my husband snapped at me.

I looked over at him to see tears flowing down his face. I guess I didn't see the surprise in it all because I'd known the entire time. It was his fault he didn't believe me!

He got up from his chair and came to hold my hand, his entire body trembling.

"Let me take these to the doctor!" The ultrasound tech left the room.

"What's wrong? Aren't you excited?" I didn't really understand his reaction. The babies were healthy and growing perfectly.

"I'm just scared. What are we going to do now?"

The rain started to sprinkle on my saddle horn as we gathered yearling cattle. Panic, my black and white painted pony, had already started with his bullshit. Yes, horses on Rush Creek had some wild names— just go with it. I'd lost two of my favorite horses at this point in my life, and I was down to the bottom of the barrel. I was seven years old, riding a horse named Panic. Panico, the freako…

The sun had fooled us all and soon began to hide behind some cumulus rain clouds. In my logical brain, I knew there was no way in hell I was getting out of this one. In my hopeful brain, I thought Dad would have mercy on me and let me ride back to the house to stay dry.

Panic veered his body away from the rain as the wind picked up and the drops increased in size. My little Levi's were quickly being saturated, and the cattle started to disperse.

Our neighbor and dear friend Kenny was there that day to help us, and I watched as the two adult riders took haste to move the cattle into the downpour. Just as my horse had done, the cattle shielded themselves from the water droplets and turned the opposite direction of the house. My rose-colored sunglasses didn't come with windshield wipers, and I was just as blinded as the animals.

Round and round we went, pushing the cattle in the most unnatural way, going against their every instinct to stay *out* of the rain. It was three riders against a few hundred head of cattle, and we were losing, indefinitely.

After many tries, we miraculously made it to the fence line where the gate was located. There was no corner to funnel them in. The gate was right in the middle, making it difficult for the cattle to find.

Several times over, we got the cattle to the fence, but they failed to locate the open area. The rain poured down furiously.

Dad and Kenny loped back and forth, rain sliding off the brims of their felt hats. The authority of their spurs and their weight got them places that I couldn't quite get to yet—like forward, for example. My Carhartt jacket stuck to my body and my ponytail pulled at my scalp with the weight of the water it absorbed. I kicked and spurred, I signaled my horse forward, and for what? My efforts were pointless. The yearlings found the fence line and hugged it as tight as a secretary's skirt. Kenny pushed from the back of the herd while Dad and I patiently waited for the babies to find the gate opening. We acted as a boundary, making our own corner to guide the cattle.

First the nose, then the first step, then the dart… The first animal had found the gate, and the rest followed.

Panic speed walked the rest of the way home in a side step, dramatically keeping his face away from the rain that was still pouring in sideways.

Dad directed me home while he unsaddled the horses, and I walked back to the house, drenched. I was a wet rat sitting inside the porch, waiting for Mom to greet me. Although I was freezing, she made sure to get a picture. I stripped my clothes in the doorway and headed straight for the shower.

I giggle every time I see that picture, because I didn't even realize the person I was becoming. As the rain poured down, I continued to ride. I had no other choice because, quite frankly, Dad didn't give me one. You know, kind of like life?

I positioned myself over the toilet, hurling first thing in the morning so I could go get something to eat. The sour taste of stomach acid tainted my tongue, and I felt helpless. There was no turning back now. No matter what happened, whether the rain poured down or I kept puking, we were in it for the long haul.

My daily routine consisted of puking in the morning and

continuing to puke all day. The amount of people who tried to tell me to eat some fucking soda crackers and drink ginger ale— each and every one was going to get knifed within the month. They had good intentions, but they were unaware that I didn't have morning sickness; I had ALL DAY sickness.

As I wiped my face, I took off my underwear because I'd once again peed my pants. My bladder was no match for the forced heaving I was doing every morning. I quite literally had fluids coming out of both ends.

"Give me all the symptoms, God, I beg you!" I mocked myself as I sat cradling the toilet bowl. I remembered vividly the conversation I'd had with God in the shower after my miscar- riage, begging Him to give me all the pregnancy pains as long as He gave me a healthy child. He was definitely listening that day.

Every morning, my sister Kylie was my saving grace. She started my ramen noodles while Josh was at work. Those were the only morsels of food I could digest. Everything else came right back up.

Over the course of three months, the sickness never let up. The entire summer, from June to August, I heaved all day long. I had to carry extra underwear around in my purse so that *when*, not *if*, I threw up, I wouldn't look like a dumbass who pissed their pants.

I was throwing up six to seven times per day on average. A few times when Josh was at work, I would tell my friend to be on call because I might need to go to the hospital to get an IV. I refused any nausea medications other than the Benadryl b6 combination my doctor had prescribed. I could suffer through the pain if it meant I could keep the babies safe from birth defects. I wasn't risking a single thing with this pregnancy.

Twelve weeks came and passed.

"Oh, it will let up soon. You'll be fine!" other women said with a smile when I told them it wasn't just morning sickness. I had hyperemesis gravidarum, which is very common in twin pregnancies. It makes pregnant women who get it constantly sick to their stomach. Some women have to be hospitalized and given IV fluids just to keep them hydrated. For some, it subsides, and for others, it continues throughout the entire pregnancy.

The out-of-control hormones my body was producing were not allowing me a break. It was easier to accept my fate and go throw up rather than waste my time on all of their stupid remedies. I. Had. Tried. Every. One.

Trying to explain my illness was useless. I smiled, waved, and then went to puke my guts up in private. I was beginning to wonder if the rain would ever let up; I mean, the puke.

Much of my life on the ranch entailed work that had to be done. The animals' lives were in our hands, and their well-being depended on us getting it done. Sometimes we did things that just flat out sucked, like moving cattle in the rain. In those moments, I experienced what it feels like to not have an option. You just had to push through it. The first half of my pregnancy, I was riding right into the rain. Each day I had my head in the toilet, I was one step closer to finding the gate to push the cattle through.

I was certain I would end the pregnancy just like I'd ended that day gathering cattle—feeling like a skinny wet rat.

CHAPTER THREE

NOVEMBER 7, 2020

My sister watched as I struggled to put on my shoes.

"Do you want help?"

"No!" I snapped back at her. The only shoes that fit me were these strappy wedge heels. I laid out a Pepcid and a b6 to prepare for my meal. I wasn't ready to have my belated birthday dinner ruined by my rearranged insides. I could hear how heavy I was breathing just to bend over to my enlarged ankles.

I hurt everywhere, and I still had until at least December. The twins were due January 28, but my doctor prepared me to go early. I tried to think about the pregnancy as one day at a time, but the thought of continuing on in so much pain and discomfort for at least two more months brought me to tears.

A medium-rare steak sat in front of me, and I looked around the restaurant, ready to roll my eyes at any judgment. I just wanted to enjoy this meal. I'd been eating ramen noodles for so long that I'd forgotten what a good steak tasted like.

"How far along are you?" a woman asked from the table next to us. I was very familiar with this question and explained that I was only around seven months along, but I was carrying twins. If

I didn't mention the twin part, it was obvious that I was much larger than the normal pregnancy.

The dinner was somewhat peaceful. I was full almost instantly, even though I was starving before we walked into the restaurant. We ordered chocolate cake, and I only ate a few bites. Josh watched me, concerned and distraught. He could tell I wasn't necessarily enjoying myself, but I was trying my best. My pregnancy wasn't fun like he thought it would be. He'd pictured us eating my cravings together and enjoying the time I had at home. I still wasn't back in the classroom because of the pandemic. Instead of taking long walks and binge-watching TV shows with me, he usually sat and watched me sleep or held my hair while I threw up what he'd made for dinner.

I heaved my body out of the chair and put my mask on to leave the restaurant. At least we got out of the house, right?

November 8, 2020

The next morning, the toilet was filled with fragments of my chocolate cake. I'd pushed it further than the Pepcid could take. I hadn't puked from pure nausea for a couple of months, but food never seemed to pass my esophagus at this point in the pregnancy. It often bubbled back up my throat, fighting the Tums, defeating them every time.

Josh took our retriever down to Monte Vista, Colorado to hunt ducks. Looking back, it seems as though we were all nesting and preparing for our boys to arrive. He knew that this would be the last time he and our dog Mattie would be able to hunt for a while once the twins were born.

I encouraged him to go. I'd just had a doctor's appointment, and everything was on track. The doctor mentioned a Christmas arrival. Although I wasn't thrilled at a Christmas birthday, it meant that I wouldn't have to be pregnant for much longer.

He left early that morning at around 3 a.m., and I found myself in the bathroom once again. This time, the toilet water turned purple from the Tums I'd taken before bed. It seemed as though the indigestion was getting worse, and the pressure from the babies was making it hard for me to breathe, even when sitting upright.

Josh promised me he was just going for the day, and I didn't have a problem with it until he was gone. For some reason, the two-hour distance really started to make me uneasy. I tried not to think about it. I started a few shows on Netflix, only to look down at my phone and wait for him to text that he was on his way home. I did my best not to bother him, but that day felt like an eternity.

My phone buzzed, a phone call rather than a text. He was driving home in a snowstorm over the La Veta Pass in southern Colorado, and the stress in his voice wasn't hidden. At that moment, I think we both knew that would be the last time he traveled that far away from me. We were getting too close to the babies coming to take risks like that.

When he got home, I was awake, throwing up my Tums again. It seemed like every night, the babies were growing enough to shove my organs out of my mouth. I sat on the floor next to the toilet crying.

"I don't think you should go far from me anymore. I can't make it much longer. I think I just want to be hospitalized." I dramatically blabbered as he watched me struggle to get off the floor. He offered his hand, but I slapped it away in frustration. I had never felt as helpless as I did that far into my pregnancy.

"I won't, hun, I had to get Mattie out before the boys come…"

November 9, 2020

Because he'd taken that day to go hunting, he was back at work the next morning. I held in my tears as he kissed me goodbye. There's something about being miserable; it really is true that it loves company. I didn't want to hurt alone, but I had no choice.

After he left, I got up to go to the bathroom. I saw a streak of old blood on my toilet paper, brown in color.

"Fuck."

I'd had discharge the entire pregnancy, so I thought it was probably normal. I didn't think twice about it as I logged into my computer to teach my first class. COVID allowed me to continue working from home even after everyone else went back to the classroom. I was a high-risk pregnancy, so my doctor's note allowed me to be miserable behind a screen in the comfort of my own home. Being miserable at home was easier than being miserable in front of everyone in a public setting. I sat in bed, trying to disguise my heavy breathing as I lectured on the cardiovascular system.

As I thought about the streak of blood, I decided I needed to call my doctor. After my first class was over, I dialed the number and waited impatiently for someone to answer. I tried to convince myself everything was fine, but I remembered that the last time I'd seen a streak of blood was when I miscarried our first baby.

"I just want to talk to my doctor. I saw him a few days ago and everything was fine, but I had some blood, and was wondering if I should come in," I told the on-call nurse. I could tell that I sounded just like all the other first-time moms. It made me realize I was probably just being overcautious. There was hardly any blood, anyway…

I finished teaching my classes, but I was just becoming more uncomfortable. There was a little bit of pain in my abdomen. I figured it was Braxton-Hicks contractions again, not the real deal labor kind. I mean, it wasn't really any different from the rest of my pregnancy. I figured it was just part of getting bigger by the hour.

I sat on my couch that evening waiting for a call back from my doctor. My stomach was tight, and the boys started to kick around as I sipped some cold water. It comforted me to feel them move, so I continued to drink more water. The TV hummed in the background, but I wasn't really watching. Instead, I was meticulously calculating all of the things that could go wrong. My phone started buzzing on the arm of the leather couch. It startled me, waking me up out of my daze.

"If your pain continues, I need you to come in to labor and delivery tonight. I'm the doctor on call," my doctor said over the phone.

On a scale of one to ten, I would say my pain was at a four, and that didn't seem serious enough to go in at 10 p.m. So I scheduled an appointment with the office for the next day, when Josh would be home and we could go together.

But the pain continued, and I was starting to wonder if something was off. How was I supposed to know? I had never done this before!

"Can you come home?" I called Josh at work, upset that I was being a chicken. I just didn't want things to get bad overnight and him not be there.

He arrived home at midnight.

By 4 a.m., I pulled out my timer. The small pains I was feeling were happening more and more frequently.

"Fuck," I whispered to myself. "Babe, I think we need to go in." I tapped him as I headed for the shower. For some reason, I felt like this might be the last time I would be home for a while.

November 10, 2020

Labor and delivery was fun. I had never been so catered to in my life. It was a calm environment early in the morning. We got there just as the new shift was arriving, and everyone seemed nice and fresh. The staff rolled out the welcome mat as we gave them our insurance information and walked into our private room. I prepared myself to be embarrassed. Surely I was overthinking this whole labor thing, and my pains were just because I was growing doubly as fast as the typical pregnant human.

The nurse hooked me up to a bunch of monitors and assured me I was probably just dehydrated. My vitals and the babies' vitals were all good. But I would be lying if I said there wasn't a little worry masked behind my relief when our vitals came back normal. The room was still on the darker side; daylight savings was in full effect. It seemed like the perfect opportunity to order some food. Again, I had this eerie feeling that shit was gonna go down soon.

Just as I started to burp up my bacon, another nurse walked in.

"I'm just going to check you really quickly while we wait for the doctor!" As she examined me, the look on her face turned grim.

"You're 90 percent effaced and one centimeter dilated. I'll get the doctor right now." She stated the medical terms that I was somewhat familiar with. That meant I was in labor, and the look on her face told me that my assumptions were right. This was not good. The thing is, I wasn't familiar with what happened next. What did they do when the babies weren't done baking?

They wheeled in the drugs.

They gave me steroids for the babies' lungs, a magnesium IV to slow my contractions, and whatever it was they stuck up my butt. Everything was happening so fast that I didn't really have time to react. I was blindsided. I'd been wishing for my pregnancy to go faster since the day it started, and I guess I finally got my wish. I kept asking God for things, and He kept giving them to me. He was just doing it in all of these crazy ways. He was also taking me way too literally. We were going to have to have another talk.

The nurse handed me a button to push every time I felt contractions. It turned out I was missing half of them. Josh was a wreck. He tried to hide it, but I could see the fear in his big green eyes. His thick eyebrows raised every time I looked at him, and although I had never known him as a little boy, that was all I could see. The desperation had unveiled him. The bald, broad-shouldered, masculine man I knew was gone.

"Kelcie, we're going to need to transport you. I have a friend in Colorado Springs, and she's going to take great care of you. We don't have the facility to have twenty-eight-week gestation babies here. I don't want you to have to be separated, OK?" My doctor explained my plan of care as he sat beside my bed.

"OK. Can he take me?" I asked, nodding my head at Josh.

"Baby, you're going to have to take the helicopter," he said. "I can't go with you…"

CHAPTER FOUR

NOVEMBER 10, 2020

THE WARM MAGNESIUM DRIP COURSED THROUGH MY VEINS as the helicopter propelled into the air. The crisp November weather had shocked my medicated body during my transport to the roof. I was thankful when the door closed. The sound was muffled now, and I was being lifted into the air. The heat from the medicine, along with the floating sensation of the aircraft, slightly distracted me from the stick in my pee hole.

I rolled my eyes doubtfully as the drugs relaxed my body, because even though my body relaxed, my uterus didn't. My already massive belly made it hard to get comfortable in the tight quarters of the helicopter, but I knew I needed a short nap. Doctors know medicine, but a woman knows her kids. This labor wasn't going to be stopped.

Eighteen minutes later, we arrived at the higher-level hospital. Somehow I had switched beds three times, and my feet never touched the floor. I was able to walk, but the staff insisted that I didn't. I called my sister as I waited for my husband to meet me there.

"Is everything OK…?" She tiptoed through the conversation, unsure how to react. She knew my tendencies, and dramatics were not what I needed right now. Everyone else would have been asking a hundred questions. That's exactly why I called her.

"Kylie, they put something up every hole of mine—my pee hole, my butthole, *and* my vagina." My words dragged out unintentionally. The magnesium they gave me made me feel so loopy.

"Gotta go, the doctors are here!" I hung up the phone. When I looked up, I realized the nurse was directing my husband into my new room. We were prepared to make this our home for the unforeseen future. It was cozy enough—for me, at least. A small part of me felt bad for my husband when I saw the couch bed in the corner of the room. It would suck for him, but misery loves company, right? Their predictions had us staying here for at least a month. The view of Pikes Peak was great. The bland hospital colors, not so much.

When the new doctor checked me, I had dilated yet another centimeter. My husband sat beside me with tears still in his eyes from his lonely drive up to the hospital. The petite female doc chirped brightly that she had dealt with this many times before, and that we had nothing to worry about.

"They're coming today," I slurred through my drugged stupor. The medications they'd given me to stop my labor were doing everything but that. My husband barked my name under his breath. My honesty was starting to scare him.

"Don't talk like that, think positive!" the doctor replied in a sharp tone. She looked at me with what seemed like surprise and anger. At that time, I had no fear; I knew that I had no choice but to be logical. My kids did things on their own time, and I was really starting to bring down the mood in the hospital room. But pregnant women are like drunk people: they always speak the truth!

I watched as the seismograph machine spiked with small earthquakes—continuous contractions of my uterus. After I had been settled for about an hour, she came back to the room. When we looked at each other, her eyes glazed over, almost as if I could see her gears turning with haste.

"Let me just check you one more time before I head to my other patient," she continued calmly as she checked my dilation a final time.

"Prep the OR. Now."

I was just so thankful we were done for the day. Stew Pedidiot walked gently down the two-track that guided us back home for the evening. I watched his pretty black mane sway back and forth as he left hoofprints in the sand. He was a beautiful bay horse, but mostly beautiful and not very smart. My left hand held the split reins, relaxed and resting on the saddle horn. The ride home was a bit different that day because Dad sat behind me on my horse, not behind me on *his* horse. We were crowded, but ole Sunny the palomino had broken Dad's reins and caused quite the uproar a few hours ago. He followed us shamefully as we made our way to cross the county road.

Dad and the hired hand visited softly, and I was content knowing we'd made it through the hardest part of the day. At least, I thought we had...

All of a sudden, Stew tucked his butt underneath him, his skin shivering beneath my legs in fear and anxiety. His ass was almost to the ground, charging up for his anticipated blowup. I responded by clenching my little legs tight against him and getting my reins secure in my hand. I was a preteen, and no matter how much I ate, my scrawny legs never got any bigger.

"I GOT IT, I got it, I got it..." I turned around to see Dad shouting at me while he carefully fished Sunny's lead rope out from under Stew's tail. His other arm was wrapped around me, and I could tell I was about to be flung. Time stood still as Dad cut the wires on a ticking time bomb. Stew stayed clenched and shaking, and so did I.

There was nothing I could do at that moment. I held my breath, waiting for my horse to calm his nerves. I had faith in Dad, but the horse? Not so much.

"I DON'T GOT IT!" In one swift movement, Dad launched me off into the sagebrush and Stew blew up, running away in fear. Ropes under your tail are apparently equivalent to torture devices. We didn't name him Stew Pedidiot for no reason, folks; he lived up to it.

The reins whipped between my legs right down the crotch of my pants as Stew ran away. Dad had been thrown and landed in the dirt. The horses stared at us in confusion as we both got up, assessing the damage. Other than feeling like I'd just had my crotch flossed with leather, I was OK. I looked up as I walked back like there was a corn cob stuck up my ass. Dad was laughing.

"Well that escalated quickly." He giggled at me while I tried to hold back a smile.

Life is unpredictable, and the ranch definitely didn't shield me from that truth. I saw firsthand how often nature can surprise you, and it was evident that it wasn't always in your favor. We did our best on Rush Creek to avoid catastrophic storms, but there's only so much in this world you can control. The day we got thrown off our horse was just one example of how nature and animals have minds of their own; they do what they want regardless of the training and the planning.

My doctors had monitored my high-risk pregnancy under a microscope. I was in pain, I couldn't eat, and I couldn't move, but on paper, I was healthy as a horse. The boys were too! Subconsciously, I'd known that I wasn't going to make it to full term. Throughout my entire pregnancy, they were in the eighty-ninth percentile in growth. They were big boys, and my uterus, only twenty-eight-weeks pregnant, was already the size of a full-term pregnancy.

I knew that they were coming, and I didn't need people to ease my mind. I needed people to be real with me. I was going to have my boys three months early, and it was going to be hard.

"I GOT IT! I GOT IT!" the doctors continued to say. When they finally listened to me and checked my dilation, I think it was much like that day riding home.

We were all about to get thrown from our horse, and I, yet again, was going to feel like my crotch had just been flossed by leather.

Only this time, it was no laughing matter.

CHAPTER FIVE

NOVEMBER 10, 2020

When my doctor told her team to prep the OR, I knew my predictions were correct. Baby A's water had burst. My boys were coming, hell or high water. Health care professionals flooded my "calm" bed rest room and got to work. They were like worker ants, shuffling all over my room, pushing equipment, directing orders, and doing it all so swiftly. The ultrasound technicians rushed into the room and squirted the jelly on my belly in a fashion that wasn't as soothing as I remembered from the first time I saw my boys on the computer screen.

"Baby A, head down. Baby B, head down. Both babies are head down!" The technician nodded to my doctor.

I'd gone over this with my OB a few months ago. I remembered the drill. If Baby A was head down, we would try a vaginal birth, and Baby B could possibly need an emergency C-section. No way to tell which way that would go until we were there in that moment. All twin deliveries are done in an operating room for that reason. If something went wrong, they had to be ready to perform emergency surgeries.

"Is it too late to get an epidural?!" I asked in fear. I was so worried that I would have to be put under if Baby B needed the

C-section. I had done my research on twin deliveries, and I did not want to miss seeing my babies for the first time.

"We're getting the anesthesiologist as we speak. Everything's going to work out just fine. We have the NICU doctor coming in to speak with you while we prep the OR," the nurse tending to me said with such compassion for my wishes.

Josh got into his scrubs, ready to enter the operating room. The NICU doctor on shift walked in, sat down in front of us, and crossed his leg over his knee as he spoke about how they treated premature babies in the NICU. At this point, my teeth were chattering. I couldn't stop my body from shaking. I wasn't sure if this was what labor felt like, or if it was from all the drugs they'd pumped into me. I could barely focus on what he was saying. The calm I'd had earlier was gone. I was so afraid of what would happen to my boys. I looked over at Josh, and he still had tears rolling down his face. The doctor told us our boys were very early: twenty-eight weeks and five days, to be exact. They most likely wouldn't be breathing when they were born, and they would be intubated and put on a breathing apparatus. We could expect them to be in the NICU until their due date—two and a half months away.

It was all so much information. The hospital staff had just told me a couple of hours ago that I wouldn't be giving birth for a few weeks, and now I was getting ready to give birth in a few minutes. Why couldn't they just be honest from the beginning? I'd told them this would happen!

They rolled me into the bright operating room. Again with the white rooms! The walls screamed at me, and the noise made it hard for me to see. I looked to my left, where two incubators were ready to take my boys away. Each incubator had a team of three people: a nurse, a doctor, and a respiratory specialist. I will never forget the sight of all six people standing there. They welcomed me with their eyes, because with masks on, that was all I could see. They were strangers, but it felt like I had known them my whole life. There were four other people on my team, including two nurses, my doctor, and an anesthesiologist. If you added me, my husband, and the boys, there were fourteen people in the room where I gave birth.

I looked up at my nurse and asked why it was so hot. The light above her head hit me hard. That was the last image I saw until I woke up to the anesthesiologist waving an alcohol swab in my face. I had passed out.

My poor husband.

Luckily I hadn't missed the birth of my children, and I was still able to get the epidural. They turned me around and I winced in pain. With every move I made, I could feel the pee stick they'd put in me hours ago. Every time I moved or contracted, the bugs crawled beneath my skin.

"Sit with your feet at the edge of the bed and lean forward," the arrogant anesthesiologist directed me. I did as he said, groaning and angry. I couldn't sit right because of the catheter. I felt like I was going to jump right off the bed. It was a combination of pain and heebie jeebies I'm sure only some people understand.

"Do you have scoliosis? Your back is kind of crooked for this epidural," the anesthesiologist asked me. The nurse directly in front of me glared back at him with beautiful piercing blue eyes. The look in those icy blues was primal. Facing forward, protector mode engaged, she was ready to pounce. I thought she was going to kill him with that one look, but before she could say anything, I chimed in.

"This fucking catheter!" I gritted my teeth, snapping back at the anesthesiologist. The nurse held me in her arms, and I felt a pinch. I knew the ten-inch needle was being inserted into my back. If I had to have an emergency C-section, I would be awake now.

"Start pushing the Pitocin," the doctor directed.

I truly had no idea what I was doing. Obviously, I had never given birth before. Although the anesthesiologist was an arrogant asshole, he was good at his job. I couldn't feel anything. I wasn't sure if I should push, or how to push, or what to do. No matter how many births in the animal world you've witnessed, you'll never know what it's like until you get to that moment.

"It's like pooping!" the nurse holding my leg said in a cheer-leader kind of way. She was so sweet, and I don't know what I would have done without her that day.

Within a few minutes, Baby A entered the world. To my surprise, he was crying. He was so tiny, and his cry reminded me of a small kitten. He was crying. He was *breathing*. I wish I could say this was a beautiful moment for me, but it wasn't. I was just so relieved that he was *breathing*. They showed me my first born, and I told them to get him to his incubator. I'd birthed one premature baby safely, and I was focused on the next. They asked if Josh wanted to go with him or stay with me. He looked at me, I looked at him, and all we did was nod as he followed Baby A out of the operating room. I didn't know I could love that man more than I did before.

I was ready to birth Baby B, but he wasn't even close. He had so much room now that his brother wasn't crowding him, I'm sure he was pretty cozy. They had to wait to give me more Pitocin. We waited, and we waited some more. It was nice to get a break, but my teeth wouldn't stop chattering. An hour passed, and they pushed more Pitocin. I pushed too. An hour after Baby A was born, his younger, bigger brother entered the world, and he was crying too. Both my boys—my boys who they'd said wouldn't be breathing—were crying. I knew at that moment that they were going to move mountains one day.

After the boys were born, they took care of me and got me into my hospital bed. My epidural wore off as quickly as it had kicked in. I tried to disregard what an asshole my anesthesiologist was because he'd worked a miracle with my pain management. The mental exhaustion set in, but there was also physical relief. I was so light. I could breathe. I'd forgotten what it felt like to really breathe. My organs let out a sigh of relief. They were free from crowding. My chest was no longer burning, my stomach no longer turning, and my pee hole…completely stick free. My body was damaged, but it still felt better than any part of my pregnancy. That's why I got up without the nurses' permission. I couldn't explain to the nurse how liberating it felt to walk to my wheelchair. She looked at me in horror as I disregarded her directions.

Josh had already met the babies while they were taking care of me and making sure I didn't bleed out. After I was done, he wheeled me into the NICU room, and there were my three-pound babies, hooked up to monitors and noninvasive ventilators. They weren't required to have a tube down their windpipes, which was a positive for us, since those tubes can be hard on babies. Instead, each of them had a nose piece that kept constant air flow to their premature lungs. They were drinking three milliliters of my milk every three hours. They were supposed to be warm and snug inside of me, but they were out taking on the world despite the circumstances.

I burst into tears in front of the NICU nurse. The hormones, along with the guilt, overtook me. It was my fault they were born so early. What if I had just gone to the doctor sooner? What if I had taken my pain more seriously? There were so many what-ifs that refused to stop playing with my mind. My heart and my mind ached, but my body was ready to face our journey ahead.

That night, I slept well. I could move my body. I could breathe. I didn't have flames coming up my esophagus anymore. Even the frequent visits from the staff didn't bother me. Helping hands were much more welcome than puking up Tums in the middle of the night. I was also trying my best to pump milk for them to take down to the NICU.

I will never forget how fast peace overcame me in my hospital bed. I went from anxiety and guilt to feeling much stronger. I reflected underneath the warm blankets the nurses pampered me with. I knew those were God's babies. When I made that realization, my mind and my heart were able to relax. I had no control over the circumstances of my labor and delivery. He knew what was happening, and so did all of my angels. Just as God had chosen me to be His cowpoke on the ranch, He had chosen me to be the mother of my two baby boys.

We had a long journey ahead of us, but that night, I just needed rest.

CHAPTER SIX

NOVEMBER 11, 2020

THE DAY AFTER THE BOYS WERE BORN, I TRIED TO WALK down to the NICU. I thought I had graduated from the wheelchair, but my angry uterus decided otherwise. We only had a few hallways to go when I folded over by the St. Francis statue at the NICU entry. I wasn't a very devout Catholic, but I remembered learning something about him. I made a mental note to look him up when we went back to my hospital room.

"I told you I would get you a wheelchair!" Josh lectured as he helped me to the ledge. St. Francis looked down on me, his eyes lecturing me just like my husband.

The closer I got to the NICU, the more my stomach started to cramp. The biological things that were happening to my body were endearing, and also just plain weird. I waved, embarrassed when the hospital staff and other NICU parents walked by. I was just sitting there in a diaper, milk leaking all over my gown. There wasn't much fabric between my butt cheeks and the cold ledge.

It was an awkward wait with St. Francis, and I was uncomfortable because I wasn't sure I had the strength to see my boys again. The night before had been emotional, and I just wanted to be steady. But the feeling of guilt still rushed over me; this all could have been prevented if I had just gone to the doctor earlier. I felt so stupid and inexperienced. Once again, I found myself in the world of my own mind, and it could sometimes be a very degrading place. I'd blamed myself for the miscarriage, and now I was blaming myself for the preterm labor. Why couldn't I make my emotional brain understand what my logical brain was thinking?

Josh came around the corner with the silly wheelchair. It brought me out of the depths of my own thoughts and I plopped my hollow body into the plastic seat. It was just as hard and cold as the ledge I was just sitting on.

I couldn't remember which rooms they were in when we checked in at the NICU desk. Before I could say anything, Josh blurted the two room numbers out and pushed me into the wash area. Since I wasn't quite used to the protocol yet, I followed Josh's lead as he washed his hands and put his phone under the germ light. I still wondered if they even worked. Josh handed me two vials of breast milk I'd pumped earlier as he adjusted his face mask. We were finally ready to go see our boys again.

They took up two NICU rooms, and a nurse met us at the door to see Baby A, my first born by an hour. Their bodies were not ready for this world yet. They lay there, still a little furry from the womb, covered in the lanugo that helps protect them during gestation. I guess I'd forgotten about that since taking Human Anatomy 201. I'd never expected to see a baby that was supposed to still be inside developing. Their little arms and backs were so hairy, it was like I had given birth to little monkeys.

I tried to hide my pain as I examined the feeding tube, the noninvasive breathing machine, and the IVs in their little arms. The alarms and beepers seemed to get louder, and my breathing became audible in my head. I didn't realize I was crying as I leaned over the incubator. The cramps hit me again, and I had to sit back down in that stupid wheelchair.

I watched as Josh followed the nurse and took care of our

kids. I didn't even know if we were allowed to touch them yet. He changed their diapers, checked their temperature, and asked questions about their latest update from the doctor. He was so happy and in the zone. I guess I'd never realized that when you're a mother, that feeling of responsibility starts right away when there's life growing inside of you. A father doesn't quite understand until they're out in the world. I admired Josh as he took the lead, but I also related to how helpless he'd felt my entire pregnancy. I felt so useless just sitting there watching, frozen by my emotions.

"I want to leave, babe," I whispered under my breath.

"Are you OK?" Josh looked concerned and fearful for me.

"Just get me out of here, please," I whispered shortly. I wasn't a fan of putting my emotions on display, and the nurse in the boys' room was standing right there as I sat in my very vulnerable state. I could still feel the lidocaine spray they'd given me to put in my bulky diaper. My body, now an empty vessel, felt dirty and uncomfortable. It felt wrong for me to be doing this in a public setting, basically naked, scared, and upset. A few hours ago I'd lain spread eagle in an operating room in front of these people, but the mental breakdown I was about to have somehow seemed more embarrassing.

I traveled to both rooms to tell the boys goodbye. I put my hand over each of them, letting them know I loved them.

When we got to my room, I sobbed as I pumped single ounces of milk into the NICU-labeled bottles. I'd failed them already. They were here, in this NICU prison, because of me. As family and friends called to check in, I lied, explaining that there was not a thing to worry about. The way the false information so easily left my lips was disturbing, but there was no sense in anyone else going through this with me and Josh. It was hard enough to deal with our own emotions, let alone everyone else's. I didn't want to hear anyone feel sorry for me, because I was already swimming in my own guilt; doggy paddling, to be more accurate.

The following weeks in the NICU were traumatic for me, and I don't know if any other NICU mom would admit to that. It's something we try to be tough through for our babies, but it takes a toll on us mentally.

I was released within forty-eight hours of birthing the boys. I looked at the "bed" in their room and listened to the constant alarms going off. There was no way in hell we were going to sleep here. Instead, we drove back and forth every day to ensure we would sleep at night. It was important for me to keep my mental and physical health in check so I could produce enough milk for both of them and support my husband through our journey. He used his sick leave in order to travel back and forth to the hospital. The fire department was rampant with COVID, and we wanted to avoid exposures at all costs. Every night, we left them an hour away from our front door in Colorado Springs. And every night, I had the same empty feeling when we said goodbye.

Our drives ranged from anger and rage to delirium and hope. The alarms on their monitors were so familiar that we often repeated them to each other in a joking matter, recalling what each one meant. *Beep boo, beep boo...*

The Brady alarm still haunts me. It was like losing a life in a video game, the sound getting lower and slower as their heart rates and oxygen levels dipped. Every time that alarm went off, the entire floor of medical staff came running. When I first came home, I would dream of that alarm going off, waking up in a postpartum sweat.

This was our new normal. Beepers, medical staff, crying, yelling, and the occasional mental breakdown—it was becoming natural. There was not a single thing we could do other than love them and wait.

The days we spent in the NICU changed me as a person. I talk about my experience often (maybe too much) but it definitely opened my eyes to the person I would become as a mother. When I met these small humans, I had to make a choice. Who was I going to be for them?

I looked up St. Francis on our way home one night, the giant statue staring me down as we left the hospital. It reminded me of sitting beneath him earlier that month. He was the patron saint of animals and the environment. Up until writing this, I'd never really thought twice about it, but now I'm starting to see a little meaning behind his watchful eye.

He probably knew a thing or two about God's Country.

CHAPTER SEVEN

NOVEMBER 2020

THE NICU WAS PREEMIE BOOT CAMP, AND WE DOVE RIGHT into caring for our babies. We had exactly a week before anyone was allowed to hold the babies or lift them out of their incubators, so we did anything else we could to feel involved in our boys' lives. Keeping their small bodies from being jostled around was crucial to prevent any brain hemorrhaging. So we became students of the nurses, learning each day how to take care of our progressing preemies.

My hands entered the two holes of the incubator as I prepared to take care of my baby for the first time. The nurses called it care time, and it took place every three hours. Between care times, we were told that the babies didn't need to be touched. They needed to rest, develop, and grow. I lifted the tabs to the preemie diaper that still swallowed my tiny guy. I wiped with ease and replaced the diaper, folding it down so it didn't ride up to his armpits. I swiftly moved his pulse ox over to the other foot, being careful not to put it on too tight. The tape wrapped around his little foot twice, and the red light was lined up perfectly to get his oxygen readings. *OK, moving on.* I put the large temperature probe in his armpit until it beeped, the nurse looking at me for the reading.

"98.8," I answered her look.

She scribbled away in her notes.

The behavior evaluator watched as I cared for him, directing me to confine his body. I listened to her and held my hand under his feet to ensure they stayed close to his body. They'd explained that preterm babies are used to being snug as a bug inside the womb, so it's important to keep them from flailing about. The calories they consumed needed to be used to grow and develop, not wasted on unnecessary movement.

Once I was finished with care time, I swaddled him, wrapping his slender arms next to his face. Hand hugs were encouraged, but no patting or rubbing. It was strange, because a mother's natural instinct is to pat them or rub their small heads in affection. Instead, Josh and I laid our hands over our babies, knowing that it would be three hours until we could do it again.

When we were done, I found myself looking at a familiar device.

The nurse unclipped the feeding tube and allowed me to drip three milliliters of breast milk down the pipe. The syringe acted as a funnel.

I watched the small amount of milk quickly empty out of the syringe.

The baby calf lay on the barn floor, almost lifeless, until I saw his eyelids blink. We'd rescued him from the cold, and his future didn't look promising. He was a little Charolais bull, white in color and large in size. Usually I would work my magic, bottle feeding the baby until he was well again.

Except he wouldn't eat. He couldn't eat.

The oversized baby bottle was warm in my arms, fogging the

air when I opened it to add the formula. The smell always made me want to gag. It reminded me of sour milk, so I held my breath as I quickly scooped the powder into the bottle. I held the bottle between my knees as I used all the strength in my skinny fingers to secure the rubber nipple over the top. While I shook the formula together like an old pro, Dad entered the barn, facing me and the struggling baby.

He held the drench. The funnel was constructed out of an old plastic liter Coke bottle, with clear tubing connected to the end. Imagine the beer chugging contests at college parties—it looked just like one of those contraptions.

I had seen Dad do this maneuver many times, but I never got used to how painful it looked. He would open the calf's lifeless mouth and aim the tube down its esophagus. I stood watching, keeping my entire body still. I wanted to be sure Dad could hear. He would put his ear in the funnel, listening to make sure the tube had gone down the correct pipe.

He held the funnel in the air and I took the nipple off the bottle.

"Go slow; don't give him too much at once," he directed as I used both hands to slowly tip the bottle over.

"Is he going to be OK?" I asked. I watched the milk swirl down the empty bottle. The calf's neck moved as if he was swallowing. Weird.

"I guess we'll see! He has some warm milk in his belly, so I'm sure he'll start to feel better," Dad replied.

Soon the rest of the bottle was empty, and I watched his limp figure. He still wouldn't lift his head.

———

One week.

It had been one week since the boys were born, and the day had finally come. Today I would hold my boys for the very first time. I'd imagined this day many times before, but it was definitely not what I'd pictured. I thought they would be covered in afterbirth, the room filled with smiles. Instead, I stood with my shirt unbuttoned and leaned over the open incubator, getting as close to my little guy as possible. Our senior nurse lectured us to always perform a straight leg deadlift technique.

"Get as close to the baby as possible, put your hand under his head and torso, and hold him against you as you stand up. Their spatial awareness isn't there yet, and they could feel like they're on a roller-coaster if you grab them out of the incubator like a normal baby." I never imagined the first time holding my kids would need instruction. The nurse encouraged me as I avoided tangling the cords.

"Good, good," she assured me as I backed toward the chair.

The first time I held my babies wasn't as magical as most say. To be honest, I was terrified I would hurt them, or that their breathing apparatus would fall off. Their bodies were so fragile, so small. There were prongs that went into their nostrils to help them breathe, and there were several cords hooked up to their monitors. When I tried to look down at him, I couldn't see past my mask. The nurse gave me a mirror to see his face. His body was scrunched in the fetal position. His heart rate slowed, and I looked at the nurse with concern.

"Babies always relax when their parents hold them," she reassured me.

The doctor told us the more that we were there, and the more that we held them, the sooner they would go home. Skin-to-skin contact was our only way to bond at that time. So we became pros at care time. Our navigation through the ventilator and pulse ox was seamless. Every chance we got, we held our babies. Feedings were increasing, and less oxygen support was needed after a few weeks. Our hard work in preemie boot camp was visibly paying off.

I had been taking care of babies all my life. I knew how

durable they were, but I also knew how quickly things could take a turn for the worse. Where I come from, life and death happen in harmony with each other. It is a blessing to understand these circles of life when you get older, but it also makes you more aware.

Some of the baby calves we rescued on the ranch would survive the feeding tube. They would grow big and strong just as the other calves did, but some didn't. The Charolais calf didn't make it, and when people told me to stop worrying, it was hard for me to explain how I had seen this situation play out before. Ignorance is bliss; knowledge and experience can be disheartening.

The only thing that comforted me was knowing it was normal, even in the world of bovines, to sometimes need a feeding tube. Not everything in nature went according to plan, and that was OK.

But even then, as hard as we were working as NICU parents, and as fast as things *seemed* to be progressing, we weren't even close to going home yet.

CHAPTER EIGHT

NOVEMBER 2020

I WENT BACK TO WORK AS SOON AS I COULD, ONLY A WEEK or so after I had the boys. While we were in NICU training, I was still teaching. My principal allowed me to continue to teach online since there was really nothing else I could do while the boys were in the hospital. My students were surprised to see my face, but I think they were also relieved. Although I had taught online the entire year, I was one of the only consistent teaching styles as my colleagues were switched back and forth from remote to hybrid learning styles. The kids knew that no matter what, my face would be on the screen every day, and the expectations around assignments wouldn't change.

We were approaching Thanksgiving break, when the holiday vacations would allow me some uninterrupted time with the boys. I had plenty of time to burn, but as a working mom, you never want to burn it if you don't have to. I knew when I brought these kids home, my world would be even messier than it was at the moment. I knew I could continue to teach, so I did.

Some people probably judged my decision to keep working during the NICU stay. No one ever said anything, but I knew. My entire life ran on routine; that's how my brain has always been wired. Now that my physical body was slowly becoming mine again (other than the milking-myself-like-a-cow part), I craved some sense of normalcy. I was consistent for my students, and they were, oddly, consistent for me. They looked forward to updates on the boys' health, and they were turning in their work and emailing me about how much they missed seeing me in the classroom. It was, compared to the NICU, a breath of fresh air.

As soon as my class ended, I found myself in the family bathroom, changing my own diaper. I had a little kit I took with me to the hospital with a cleansing bottle, massive pads, and lidocaine spray. As I ripped the giant pad out of my granny panties, I thought about how strange motherhood was and how oblivious the world was to the weirdness. *I literally just taught a class, now I'm changing my diaper, and then I'm about to go take off my shirt in front of complete strangers so I can get the best skin-to-skin contact with my kids.* I just did it all like it was nothing.

I pulled up my pants, washed my hands, and grabbed my computer bag. After we took care of the boys, I would have to teach my last class before the students' lunch break. Josh was already starting on Baby A's diaper when I walked into the patient room. The nurse welcomed me.

"How was your class?!"

Clippity clop. Clippity clop. The horse hooves danced on the concrete floor of the barn. I sighed in relief when I looked up from the feed bucket I was sitting on to see Whitey. Although her name was Whitey, she was actually "perlino." Her coat was cream colored, accented by a sort of yellow off-white mane and tail. Her skin was pink, and her eyes were blue. If you didn't know any better, you'd think I was talking about the girl next door. She shoved her face into the bucket of grain as Dad prepared her for the adventure ahead. He had mentioned earlier that we were just going to load up an injured bull. I knew he was trying to ease my cowpoke tension by downplaying the situation. But I also knew that if Whitey was being saddled, he wasn't doing something "easy."

If you remember, I was the right-hand little girl of a cowboy. But I wasn't necessarily into the rough and tough parts of the ranch. I was more into nature and the beauty of the environment. Dad on the other hand, well...I felt like he was a magnet for small disasters. We were definitely a yin and yang type of team. I tried to relax as he continued to prepare Whitey for the day.

Particles twinkled in the light that shone through the barn door. It was almost like you could see the smell of horsehair, horse poop, and dust. The way it complemented the sweet smell of grain, I feel like it should have been made into a custom candle. I followed the light beam to Whitey and watched in admiration as Dad prepared her for the day. He first combed her with the curry comb, taking the rough teeth and breaking away pieces of mud and dirt. The indentations the comb left were swept away when he went over it with a soft brush. With each pass behind her, he signaled with a hand over her rump and his body against her backside to reassure her not to kick him: trust. She continued to viciously eat her grain. Once she was nicely groomed, he added her saddle pad and blanket, positioning it properly starting at her withers right above her shoulders. Then, the saddle went on with a lift and a plop onto her strong, thick back. The straps were secured—first the latigo, then the back cinch. Finally, he put on the bridle as she finished the last pieces of grain in her mouth, getting some slobber on his hands. We were ready to go, and I was hopeful for a smooth moving day.

We drove until we turned off of the county road onto a two-track not too far from Rush Creek, the moving water that gave our ranch its name. The bull was injured with a bum leg, so he hadn't gone far from where Dad had seen him the day before. *Bob and Tom* radio comedy played in the background as we drove the old maroon pickup to gather the beast. Whitey rode in the stock trailer, awaiting her task for the day. It didn't take long to find the black bull. He was lying there looking somewhat helpless, but I knew better.

Bulls are notorious for being testosterone-pumped meatheads. If you've ever been at a bar past midnight, you know exactly how an uncastrated male bovine behaves. But these are not mere men hyped up on whiskey and bad decisions. Bulls can weigh over two thousand pounds. I've seen them move and dent vehicles. I've seen them destroy barbed wire fences. I've seen them bend metal-paneled corrals with little to no effort. And if you've seen the movie *8 Seconds*, you know that bulls can also be lethal to the brave men and women who interact with them.

I watched the black bull in disgust as Dad unloaded Whitey from the trailer. He lay there, his neck the circumference of a whiskey barrel, his body muscular and burly. Green poop was smeared over his backside, sprinkled with flies for an extra touch of nasty. He smelled of musk and machismo, and it was hard for me to feel bad for him. I knew his injury was most likely self-inflicted, maybe from trying to jump a fence or fighting with a fellow bull. He couldn't help but be powered by the hormones that coursed through his veins. The instinctual need to be with his lady friends was a fault he unfortunately could not control.

Dad slung his leg over Whitey, giving an exaggerated groan as he steadied in the saddle. He was trying to lighten the mood, because I wasn't convinced this would be easy like he said it would. Whitey, in true "bad bitch" fashion, was ready to roll. She waited in anticipation as Dad prepared his rope for battle. She was a stout mare, with the ass-end the size of a caboose. Standing 14.2 hands tall, or around 4.7 feet, she was considered a fairly small horse. At first glance, she wasn't impressive, but whoever thought that obviously had never seen her work. And man did she work. She wasted no time approaching the bull, taking short choppy steps, always moving with such haste no matter the occasion. The hot sun scorched the bull's smooth black hide, and it accentuated his muscular physique. I watched from the safety of the pickup as Dad threw a quick loop over the bull, and the work began.

I was hopeful that this was going to move quickly. Dad slowly led the bull to the trailer. The beast limped and groaned, getting closer and closer to the edge of the stock trailer. Could it be? Was he going to load that easily?

Nope.

The bull saw the end of the trailer and stopped in his tracks. In one swift move, Dad worked his rope over the trailer hook, using it as leverage against the bull. He turned Whitey around to face the beast. It was now a tug-of-war between the animals, and neither one was giving in any time soon. Dad secured his rope on the saddle horn and lightly pulled back on the reins, even though Whitey didn't really need instruction. She had already engaged her glutes and hamstrings, posting up and preparing to load the bull. The bull dug his front feet into the ground in protest. Both animals faced each other, and IT. WAS. ON.

Whitey started to step backwards, pulling the rope tight, the tension between the two animals testing the strength of the fibers. One step at a time, she took her small frame and worked the beast. He did not budge.

She continued to pull.

The bull was struggling to breathe, but he wasn't giving in just yet. His bulky limbs and his humped back were solid as a rock as he continued to fight her. After what seemed like forever, he decided to lie down. This wasn't ideal either. Were we going to lift him into the trailer?! I think not! Dad cued Whitey with his feet to move forward to let him catch his breath. The bull was so exhausted that he sprawled out his front legs and panted, still determined he would not load into the trailer.

After he caught his breath, we tried again. And again. And again. And then I heard my name…

"Kelcie! Get the HotShot!" Dad shouted.

"Daaaaaad?!" I answered back nervously.

"He's not going anywhere! Stay behind the trailer gate!" Dad shouted even more.

I knew this was going to happen. I scurried into the back of the pickup and grabbed the HotShot, a little prod that produces a shock to get cattle moving. I tested the button, the *bzz bzz* noise reassuring me it worked. I shuffled behind the trailer gate to the nasty bull butt. He was still fighting us. At this point the bull was done physically, but the sheer poundage he carried made it impossible to move him. I applauded his persistence, because he was not going to get in that trailer. I clenched my teeth in anticipation as I gave him the HotShot to the butt. He didn't give a shit.

"Get 'em again!" Dad yelled, startling me. So I gave him a few more buzzes to the butt. Still nothing. I wanted to give up.

Whitey continued to pull the rope.

She had been holding the rope solid this entire time. Sweat was running down her flanks, and the dirt hidden in her hair had started to solidify into mud streaks in her creamy white coat. Dad stepped off Whitey, and instead of letting up, she continued to take small steps back.

She kept pulling.

This bull was not going anywhere on her watch. I had no idea what my dad had planned at this point, but at least he was going to help me with this butt buzzing business. The saddle started to peel off Whitey's back. The latigo was starting to wedge in her armpits. She dug her feet into the dirt and put her head down toward the ground. I thought the rope was going to pull the saddle over her head.

She kept pulling.

Dad was much braver than I and got close to the bull, making noises, *buzz buzzing* with the HotShot, and trying to nudge him with the gate to get him into the trailer. The bull huffed and puffed, his hot breath heating the already warm summer air in front of him. He finally took a step up into the trailer.

Whitey kept pulling.

With a big *clop, clop, clop*, the bull trampled into the trailer.

She kept on pulling.

Dad ran and shut the gate before the bull could escape.

All the while, Whitey never stopped pulling the rope.

There were a lot of people who felt bad about what I was going through. They pitied me as I worked while riding the emotional roller-coaster of a NICU stay. My immediate family was different, though. They knew me well, and they never questioned my decisions. I had been this way all my life. As the firstborn daughter of three kids, I grew up holding down the fort. I knew what I needed to do. So I continued to teach, just as Whitey had continued to pull the rope. Sympathy was the last thing I wanted.

Everyone on the ranch had their job. In that moment, when Whitey was handling that bull, it was very clear what her job was. The trust I had in that horse to keep us safe is something I still can't explain. I didn't question her one bit. Teaching was my job, and it was one of the only things I could do at that moment to keep my sanity. It was the perfect distraction from the intrusive thoughts. It gave me routine and familiarity. Because if I wasn't teaching, I was resenting every woman who got to take her kids home with her. Because if I wasn't teaching, I was allowing the guilt to lurk back into my brain and take over.

I needed my job. It was the most consistent thing I had through the entire pandemic.

Thanksgiving and Christmas break gave me some time to be distraction free during our NICU stay, but I continued to teach. The bond my high school students and I had that year was strong. They knew the mental load I had taken on, and I knew what they were going through as well.

I taught on my couch between pumping sessions.

I kept teaching.

I taught in the car on the way to the NICU.

I kept teaching.

I taught in the waiting room, and I taught on the NICU couch, my students quickly becoming used to the background noise of the beepers.

I continued to teach.

CHAPTER NINE

"Fuuuuuuuuck!!!"

I slammed my hands repeatedly on the dash of our Envoy. "It isn't fair. IT. ISN'T. FAIR!" Josh looked at me in fear. I'd filled our entire NICU stay with toxic positivity, pushing his feelings back down his throat any time he felt upset. I wasn't really allowing either of us to let out any emotion. The universe seemed to work in mysterious ways with me, and I didn't want to let any of those thoughts jinx my kids. But I was full of rage, wondering why *I* had to go into preterm labor. I wondered why *we* had to leave our babies every evening while others got to have them at home. It felt like if I let one ounce of negativity slip, something bad would happen to our boys. Our luck would run out if we weren't careful.

But I couldn't keep the feelings down forever.

I screamed again, angry tears rolling down my face. My body did nothing but convulse with unnatural breaths that somehow kept me alive.

It wasn't what had happened that day; it was what had happened every day up until that point.

The constant attention I was under because of our situation

grated uncomfortably against my introverted personality. I knew in my heart that they meant well, but the constant influx of texts every day from people who'd never experienced what I did just made my anxiety around our NICU stay worse.

When they're five pounds they can come home!
When can they come home?
When can they come home?
When can they come home?

It's amazing how many people asked me that question, knowing damn well I was asking the same one. The boys couldn't even eat without a feeding tube at the time of my mental breakdown, let alone breathe on their own without oxygen.

A lactation nurse had worked with me that day and lectured me on how to hold the baby, how to hold my boob…

"And don't depend on the monitors, watch your baby!" she nipped at me (no pun intended).

The directions continued to overwhelm me, and I felt like my blood was going to boil over and shoot out my ears. She kept barking orders—*do this, do that.* And I had to do it twice because I had two babies to feed who, by the way, ate in completely different styles. Not to mention that the oxygen cords and the feeding tubes and the monitors all tangled up in that ugly hospital recliner made me feel like I was going to blow. I looked around, searching for a way to escape. I was trapped.

I could smell my armpits, something they told me was part of postpartum. My arms were sticking to my sides. The blankets and cords were starting to overwhelm me. I would have run, but I knew the oxygen would yank me and the baby back into the grasp of the NICU room before I could get as far as the door.

My teeth gritted underneath the mandatory mask, and my eyes went blank. The only way for me to get through this was to disassociate. If I didn't, I would be crying within minutes.

We were at the phase where the boys needed to be exposed to both bottle and breast to practice eating on their own. It was one of their last and final tests before we got to go home. I looked up at Josh, his eyes looking back at me in desperation and love. He had no idea how to help me, and I tried not to hate him for not having boobs. He later bottle fed the boys after our failed attempts at breastfeeding. Breastfeeding was something I'd really wanted to do, but it was supposed to feel natural. This shit—with the cords and the monitors and the woman maneuvering my boob—was not natural.

After the fiasco, we swaddled the twins and left them to the care of the hospital. We were on our way home. One day of hell closer to being home with my kiddos.

I could hear my heart beating inside my head as we walked out of the NICU. I'd held back my explosion until we got in the car. As soon as we turned out of the hospital parking lot, I completely lost it.

It wasn't fair.

I cringed, sympathy pain for the cow that was being lifted into the air by our HydraBed pickup. The chain hooked up to her allowed us to maneuver the cow who'd just given birth.

A prolapsed birth.

Her entire uterus was on the outside of her body now.

The sex education I received on the ranch was more useful than any book they presented to me in school. I was up close and personal with a womb that had just carried a baby calf for months. It was bright in color, pink, and covered with tiny purple raisins—little nodules that looked like brains.

"Lift her up, Kelc," Dad directed me as he rolled up his sleeves. I pressed the button located under the steering wheel of the pickup.

"Alright! That should be good!" I hopped down from the pickup seat and ran to the back, where Dad was getting ready to "operate." I was directed to control the clean water. Dad washed his hands and his arms before he started to work on her.

"Those little brain things are where the baby gets its nutrients from," Dad explained as he started to push the uterus back into the cow's vagina. She hung from the HydraBed, helpless. He continued to wash water over her uterus as he pushed it back in. My job was to help him wash his hands continuously. He wanted to keep his hands clean, keep everything he could out of the mama cow.

Once the uterus was back in place, I thought we were done, but Dad pulled out a massive needle and baling twine. He slowly stitched up her vagina, a barrier to attempt to keep her uterus inside.

"Is she going to be OK, Dad?"

"Probably not," he answered shortly, his eyes focused on his stitches.

"Well, why are we doing this then?"

"Well Kelc, the boss wants us to try to keep them all alive. If we have to take her to the sale, we take her to the sale."

I shut up for the rest of the procedure.

It hurt to watch. After the cow had her baby, she became chopped liver. She'd just offered up the biggest sacrifice and the biggest gift all in one day, only to be hanging there while we attempted to extend her life for—what, a few weeks? A month?

I could tell Dad was irritated, and so was I. Although I was only in grade school, that moment stuck with me into my adult life.

"It's going to be OK, mama," Dad said as he sewed her up.

Emotionally, the NICU stay had taken me to the darkest place of my life. Repeatedly leaving my babies in a hospital every night turned me into a lobotomized zombie. My body was there, but the emotions continued to stay masked under all the stress I was under. The day I lost it in the parking lot, I felt so helpless. I imagined that mama cow hanging there, an empty vessel. That was exactly how I felt: empty.

My hate and resentment were probably the only thing that got me through the NICU stay. You could say I prayed to God, but I think for the most part I was yelling at Him, questioning why He continued to put me through hardships I didn't deserve. It sounds ass-backwards, but somehow, my anger toward the situation got me *through* the situation. It helped hide my real feelings, and it kept my family and friends from bothering me. If I could stay cool as a cucumber in front of them, I didn't have to deal with the sympathy talks or the uncontrollable crying. Running on anger and rage was a lot easier than letting the sadness and guilt I was really carrying overcome me.

The selfishness of my postpartum fog would not lift. It didn't feel fair that others got to come home with their children. It didn't sit right with me that they continued to complain about how hard it was. It infuriated me day in and day out, so badly that I had to stay off social media. Any image of kids at home with their parents sent me into a hateful rant at God every time.

Another woman texted me to ask how I was doing once. Her child was a few months older than the boys. When I asked how she was doing, she told me that she wasn't sleeping and went on to complain about the newborn phase. All I could say was…

At least he's home with you.

All women deserve to feel valid in their experience as a mother, but at that moment, only my experience mattered. All my life, I was there for anyone who needed it, but at this juncture, I had no time for anyone else's problems. Mine felt like they were the most important.

The woman I had become since my cowpoke days accomplished anything and everything. But this was one thing in my life that I had zero control over, and it was frying my brain into a mental comatose. The ranch had taught me that grit and hard work can get you almost anywhere, but it wasn't going to do shit for me right now.

God had those kids taken care of, and He watched as I failed to trust Him. That moment in my life made me realize that as soon as I brought children into this world, I was no longer in control. The wheels were off the rails, and we were no longer playing by my rules.

We were playing by theirs, and I was probably going to be losing most of the time.

If you're anything like me, winning has been ingrained into your brain. You can probably see how this was a hard pill for me to swallow. The cowpoke I had become on the ranch later grew up to be a hard young woman. Whether academically or financially, I would brute force smash through any obstacle in my path. This was different, though. Bringing children into the world meant surrendering to the obstacles they brought on.

As we pulled out of the hospital, I didn't want anyone to fix the situation. I thought of that cow hanging there from the HydraBed. She had no control over what had happened. All she could do was *be*. The situation sucked, but Dad still comforted the animal. And now, all we could do was what we could do, but I remembered those words he'd whispered to the cow. Those words were the only thing I wanted to hear.

"It's going to be OK, mama."

CHAPTER TEN

JANUARY 16, 2021

My evenings leading up to the day the boys came home consisted of cleaning the house and shopping for things I would need when they arrived. We'd already had a baby shower in October, knowing that the boys were going to be early, so I was able to complete the finishing touches two months postpartum. That was one positive of the whole thing. I even started their baby books, giving me something to keep my mind occupied while they prepared to come home.

Josh and I went out to eat a few times, enjoying our last days as just *us*. I was thankful for our time together. It was the "babymoon" we never got to have while I was miserable and pregnant. We went shopping, gorged ourselves at our favorite restaurants, and watched television shows before we called the evening nurse to see how our boys were doing. It was the calm before the next storm.

On the sixty-seventh day in the NICU, January 16, 2021, they gave the medical release for my babies to come home. Although exciting, this day was the true beginning of my wild ride as a twin mama. The anticipation of coming home had been driving us crazy. Now, it was here. The longest days of my life were abruptly ending, and I wasn't sure how to react. They were coming home!

They were coming home?!

When I heard the diesel engines, I looked out my bedroom window to see the old pickup trucks rolling down the driveway. Stock trailers trailed behind with all the ranch ponies ready to work. The clatter of their hooves transitioning from the trailers to dirt mixed with the sound of good morning chitchat.

After I buttoned my britches, I headed into the kitchen to check out Mom's progress on the meal. The roasters, crockpots, and oven were stoked. The aroma of a big hunk of brisket filled the air. Mom's homemade bread was rising on the stove waiting for its turn in the oven, and she had all the salads crammed in our fridge, ready to feed the army that came to help. As I stole a piece of brisket, she directed me to make the tea. I filled a gallon jar with water and screwed the tea bag strings in with the lid. I set it on the front step and smelled the dewy air.

When Mom was done running me around the kitchen to prepare for the meal ahead, I headed down to the branding pens. She sent me with a container of donuts to feed the men and women breakfast. Cows and calves funneled into the gated area, the cowboys handling them with great ease because the mama cows were *frantic*. It was loud. They bellowed and moaned, searching for their calves, pacing the fence line waiting for their babies to be released back to them. I stood on the fence as I watched Dad hook up the propane bottle to the branding pot. He lit the flame and it roared with heat. The ranch symbols slowly started to turn red.

Syringes were turned upside down to draw vital vaccinations, knives were dragged across wet stones in preparation to castrate the males, and most of the horses were parked out of the way before the branding commenced.

Once the mamas were separated from the babies, the work began. I watched as strong, quiet horses tried their best to keep the baby calves calm. They carried their cowboys in a way that didn't make the babies any more anxious than they already were. The cowboys swung their ropes, aiming for the hind legs, learning occasionally to fish for the catch. They raised their arms swiftly, securing the loop around the hind legs. A single rope coil wrapped around their saddle horn—a dally. The horses would turn around toward the branding pot, the rope pulled tight, and it was a vision of the Western world. The cowboys sat upon their flexed horses, looking behind them, using the rope tension as a guide to keep a firm gaze on the animals' safety. The ropes indented their chaps, and their hats shaded squinted eyes.

Each calf, all five hundred of them, were roped and dragged to the ground crew. The ground crew consisted of young agile cowpokes willing to wrestle each squirrely baby. There, the babies were branded, vaccinated, and castrated. The process sounds traumatic, but it isn't much different than what a newborn human goes through at the hospital. Human babies are vaccinated, males circumcised, mucus suctioned out of their nose and mouth…it's all part of the process. The pokes and prods are all precautions to keep them safe.

Smoke billowed in the air, and burnt hair made its way to my olfactory receptors. It was a smell I would never forget. It was also a time I would never forget.

When all the calves were branded, they were released back to their mothers and the crew went to eat the dinner Mom had prepared. She worked on this ahead of time, making trips into the city to Sam's Club, buying items in bulk to feed the cowboys. Although most of the action was in the branding itself, the dinner was my favorite part.

After all the hard work was complete, the cowboys and

cowgirls would wash their hands. They smelled of burnt hair and cow shit, but it was somehow appealing. Cold beers were cracked and iced tea was poured. It was a ceremony to thank God, the land, and the cattle for their bounty. Babies were now safe with their mothers. This was the time when everyone gathered together to eat the food made with love and rejoice with good conversation.

They came out of honor and integrity.

They came out of love and comradery.

They were our village.

It all happened very quickly at the end of our NICU stay. The boys graduated from every oxygen apparatus required, and they were eating full bottles with no feeding tubes. The only other requirement was that they didn't have a bradycardic episode—when the heart rate slows due to lack of oxygen—for five days in a row. We were in a sickening countdown for about two weeks straight before they both stopped holding their breath.

Somehow, someway, they timed it perfectly to both come home on the same day. They still required oxygen tanks, so we lugged two car seats, two babies, two oxygen tanks, and the haul of diapers we'd opened while still in the NICU. We brought the Dodge Ram because Josh felt more comfortable keeping them safe in the bigger vehicle. The nurse helped us heave the massive infant seats into the pickup.

Oxygen tank, car seat, handoff.

Oxygen tank, car seat, handoff.

Sitting between the twins, I held their pacifiers and directed Josh to turn down the radio so I could hear them breathing. The hour drive home from the NICU made me nervous because we'd been released at 9 p.m. The rise and fall of their chests was not visible, and I continued to put my hand over their faces to make sure I could feel them breathing.

There were a lot of emotions in the air, but my lack of control over the situation was the number one cause of my anxiety. I never wanted to see them hooked to those machines again. I never wanted to feel the distance between us again. None of it. Never again. How was I going to protect them without worrying every second?

When we arrived home, we agreed that no one but my sister was allowed at the house until we had time to settle. She was living with us at the time, and the uneasiness of RSV and COVID made us very wary of letting anyone else near our premature babies.

"A simple cold could put them right back in the NICU," the doctor explained to us when they released us to go home. That made the decision easy.

We carefully wrapped our new roommates in swaddle burritos, placing them inside the double bassinet next to our bed. Their tiny little nostrils flared as the oxygen kept them safe from their premature lungs. So peaceful, and so perfect.

They were 2.5 months old weighing around eight pounds, the size of a normal newborn. The absence of beepers and monitors made me and Josh uneasy. How were we supposed to tell if they were alive now? For the past sixty-seven days, we'd depended on all of those pesky connections to the wall to relieve our tensions. I'd bitched about them then, but now that we were home, it was eerie. The silence wasn't as peaceful as we thought it would be. We turned the lights out, finally ready to sleep at home next to our boys for the first time.

This was it. Here we go.

A baby coughed, and we both sat up in unison.

It was going to be a long night...

We were going to need that village now.

The Western way of life is built on traditions, and it tends to build villages I like to call ranch families. I always paid attention to the way our village respected my parents. I enjoyed the feeling it gave me to see their handshakes, their compliments of the meal, and their joyful conversation. None of them would ever admit to it, but they all had a love for each other that was never spoken out loud. They weren't paid to come and help us. There was an understanding that we would be there when they needed us, just as they were for us.

When my kids came home, I quickly learned that I would need to find my village. This was unfortunately easier than I thought. I say unfortunately because when you have children, people you wouldn't expect come out of the woodwork to help, and the people you thought had your back tend to disappear.

So many people brought us meals, gave us food gift cards, took us out to dinner while we were in the NICU. I even remember one of my friends taking an entire bag of frozen breast milk to the hospital for our kids. The pandemic brought on so many challenges that parents in the past had never seen before, and parents like us were facing it head on.

The night after we brought the boys home, we thought we would keep everyone away for a few days, but we quickly texted my parents asking for mental support. What's funny is that we didn't really need their physical help; we just needed someone to sit with us and process what we had been through.

The rolling oxygen tanks tangled the room, the double array of baby containers crowded every living area, and we thought that was less chaos than the NICU. When our family came over, it was obvious that it wasn't normal. The circumstances we'd come home to were something only a fraction of the world encountered.

Although it wasn't impossible to do alone, for our mental sanity, we sought a village.

CHAPTER ELEVEN

FEBRUARY 2021

BOOM! My sister kicked down the door, one of the twins nestled in her arms. My body woke before my brain. It was only a few hours of sleep, but in my dreams, I'd forgotten I was a mom. My body, however, did not.

Kylie handed me a quiet baby. Quiet isn't always good. I looked down and saw that his face was starting to turn purple. Without a second thought, I turned him over on my forearm and gave him a heavy blow to the back.

"A small pat isn't good enough," the voices of our NICU nurses repeated in my head.

Baby B immediately gasped for air, and my stiff body relaxed as I pulled him close, his body melting into mine in comfort. He was alive. We were all OK.

Tears flowed down Kylie's face, and I was so overwhelmed by the whole situation I didn't even realize I was crying too. After all the commotion, the house suddenly seemed so quiet. It made sense since it was only around 2 a.m. Baby A slept alone in the living room; the only sounds were our sniffling.

The nurturing side of me has always been there, but it's always been hard for me to express. Though I've never been the touchy-feely type, Kylie is my sister, and what had just happened was scary.

I didn't know what else to do, so I grabbed her little sausage fingers.

"You did good. We did good," I managed to get out between sobs.

The training I'd gone through in the NICU paid off, and my sister did exactly what I'd taught her. *Watch the baby, look at his coloration, look for swallowing in his neck.* I trusted very few people with my children, but my sister? She was the real MVP.

The first month home with the twins was pure survival mode. Josh was working twenty-four hours on and forty-eight hours off at the fire department. My sister was living with us in the interim while she finished her online degree. I was off on maternity leave for exactly eight weeks. We were all suffering the wrath of preemie twins.

They were so precious, but the work that came with the package was a little bit insane and a lot bit exhausting. Their oxygen tanks were a hassle as we all tried to move through the house, especially during the night. The dishwasher never stopped running, full of my pump parts and the amazing yet annoying pieces of Dr. Brown's bottles. I felt similar to a milking cow, pumping ten to sixteen ounces per sitting. Burp rags covered the furniture. The pack 'n plays, the boppy pillows, and the bouncy chairs were scattered around the house. We'd graduated from preemie boot camp, but there was no escape from the twin boot camp we were all in.

Although they were the size of normal newborns now, the boys still came with their preemie baggage. Acid reflux kept them up in the middle of the night, their grunts like small goats. I guess I passed the indigestion on to them. We still practiced side lying feeding so they wouldn't aspirate. Instead of holding them in the crook of our arms, we laid them sideways on a pillow. It kept the milk from running straight back to their throats;

instead, it pooled in their cheeks, allowing them to slowly swallow and not choke.

We were so used to the NICU schedule that I kept them on the same routine at home. Every three hours, we changed diapers, fed them, and put them to sleep. Some called me neurotic or said I kept too tight of a schedule...but if we hadn't done this, I would have never had a second to rest. The breast pump became a part of me, and the snacks were always close by. My appetite resembled a famished pride of lions. I was only one part of the machine that kept our home running.

My sister was critical to the mechanics, and that night, with bloodshot eyes and sleep-deprived brains, she did what any good sister would do. She was there for me.

My stringy brown hair flew around me as I frantically ran around the ranch house. I was so skinny that the only pants that fit me were little stretchy leggings, and even those hung loose from my twiggy legs. I stood at the top of the concrete stairs to the cellar chucking down pillows and blankets. My bare toes grabbed at the edge of the first step. I wanted to take my mattress down there too, but Mom wouldn't let me take it off my bed. I grabbed a bottle of water, my sister's milk bottle, and my Cheetos. I didn't know how long I would be down there, so I made sure we had enough food. I grabbed flashlights, batteries, and the home phone. Mom watched as I carried my items down to the cellar in preparation for the tornado. I leaned against the wall to make my beanpole body sturdier as I struggled to hold onto everything. I really wish cell phones and cameras had been more advanced at this time. I would have loved some videos of these moments.

Mom knew the tornado wasn't terribly close, and we were never in imminent danger. But I was convinced the tornado was going to come and rip the house off the ground, forcing us to hide under all the pillows and blankets to protect us from flying debris. For some reason, the school tornado drills had convinced me that this was how my life would end.

Not in my house!

It was summertime on the plains, and my sister was still a baby. The afternoon came, and the thunderclouds rolled in. Tornado warnings scrolled across the bottom of the TV screen, and my Kindergarten Tornado Training kicked in. My uncle was the hired hand on the ranch at the time, and Dad was out driving around with him. I was infuriated with them both. They were out gallivanting in tornado weather! Kylie played on the floor of the living room while Mom cleaned in the kitchen. At the time, it really bothered me how nonchalant everyone was acting. Instead of relaxing and waiting for direction, I took charge of the situation.

Of course, by the time I got my sister to the cellar, all of the weather was gone, and thank God our house wasn't destroyed. I'd had visions of that movie *Twister* ingrained in my brain, sure that a cow would come winding around the cyclone if we looked outside to check on the thunderstorm at the wrong time. All that mattered was that I'd done what I was supposed to do. I protected my family.

What happened that day was the precursor to the rest of my life as the oldest sister. When I became a big sister in 1999, my days as an only child were over. I had moved up in the household ranks, and I took responsibility for her just as my parents did. The minute I saw her, I fell in love. I planned all the ways we were going to bond together, just like on the TV shows. I would do her hair and read books to her. I would kiss her and love her. I truly felt like she was my own personal baby doll. Little did I know that this would not be our relationship.

My sister Kylie came from another planet. She was loud, wild, and talkative. She hit me, and she stole my toys. She lit up the room with her smile. In most stories, you might think I was jealous, but to me it was more like confusion. My sister thrived on socializing and interaction. I was completely OK talking to no one and playing by myself. I realized in the early days of big sisterhood that we were nothing alike. I thought with logic and structure. Kylie didn't think, she just did! My parents created two very different girls, and with such an age difference, our relationship has always been unique. I was my parents' cautious, predictable cowpoke, and my sister was the daring, vibrant cowpoke. Our differences were meant to be vast. God created us like magnets so we would always stick together.

I was Head Cowpoke after she was born, and I had a duty to the household when Dad was gone. He never told me that, but I assumed that position on my own. It was my job to take care of my mom and my new little sister. I can still picture her on her horse, riding straight into the middle of the herd with no care in the world. I remember so vividly watching her bring baby goats back to life, and her happy-go-lucky attitude. Nothing ever fazed my sister the way it fazed me. I was always jealous and stressed out by the way she could go through life without worry.

As we got older, Kylie continued to confuse me. She didn't do chores correctly or in a timely manner. She dillydallied, and she never stopped talking. I remember lecturing her about getting tougher. I told her that one day I would be gone to college and she would have to do the chores. I told her I couldn't always be the one doing all the labor-intensive work around the ranch. She tagged along, ignoring my lectures.

I know it bothered her that I was constantly on her ass about her choices in life, but she will never know how much it pained me to see her hurt, ever. My sister went through heartaches, life decisions, and fights as she grew up. The six-year age difference made it hard for me to stand by and let it happen. I know she resents me for it. She has always had another mother instead of a sister. I've always been so hard on her, but I think it was my first glimpse of the protective mother I would become.

In the days spent living with newborn twins, I think my sister saw me at my weakest points mentally, and I could tell it bothered her to see me that way. When she sat crying in front of me that night, I knew that life had come full circle. She saw what it was like to see me in pain, and that was the moment I think our relationship changed. She saw what I had been doing this entire time. Suddenly, we were doing this thing called life together, and she wasn't just my kid sister anymore.

She was my rock.

CHAPTER TWELVE

FEBRUARY 2021

"You're a first-time parent. You'll get over that." I was becoming numb to this phrase. The programmed smile I gave people when they downplayed my worry became way too easy to put on.

I watched as a family member tipped my baby back and shoved the bottle in his mouth to feed him.

"That isn't how you do it. This isn't me being controlling—this is a safety issue." I tried to keep my tone calm, but I was barely managing not to put them in a chokehold. Luckily the helpless baby deterred me.

"I had two of my own kids. I know how to feed them," they responded.

A premature baby can essentially drown in milk if it shoots straight back into their throat. It may be a natural thing to tip a baby back and hand them a bottle, but it just wasn't natural for preemies yet.

"But you didn't have them in the hospital for sixty-seven days." Pulling out that statement usually got them to do what I asked.

In those first few months at home, family and friends made

their way through our chaotic home to visit the boys. I noticed that I was starting to filter out who was in my village and who was just there to make things harder for me. There was a clear difference between the two. The problem was, the ones making things harder thought they were being helpful.

Noses turned up when I asked for guests to wash their hands. Eyes rolled when I asked them not to kiss my babies. I watched family members ignore me when I explained how to feed a premature baby.

I never knew people had such audacity until I brought babies into the world, and man did they have the AUDACITY.

For a lot of our family and friends, it was obvious how overwhelming the situation was for them. Their faces were nervous as they held babies hooked to oxygen. I didn't realize how desensitized I was. The oxygen tank was minimal compared to what we'd had just a few months ago in the hospital.

The other half of our family and friends just couldn't grasp the severity of the situation. They weren't there when my precious boys would stop breathing, the alarms bringing in the entire floor of nurses. They didn't know how second nature it was for me to stimulate them. I had to "remind" their premature brains to breathe! And they weren't there when we were nearing the end of our NICU stay and the nurse had bad news. They didn't see her face when she told us Baby A had stopped breathing and wouldn't respond, so they had to force air into his lungs with a bag and mask. They didn't know that just five short days before coming home, my kids had had one of these "breathing episodes." It was a normal occurrence in premature babies, and we were "used" to it. At least, we thought we were.

They weren't there. They didn't know. And they still disregarded me.

They disregarded my wishes, and they disregarded the safety of my children.

My village was getting smaller.

Why am I trying out for Tiny Tot Princess? I asked myself as I mounted my horse. I didn't feel like arguing with my parents, but it was a serious question I had. Why?

I rode alone, practicing my routine in our home arena while Dad was in the barn. The two-year-old gelding acted in ways my older, more tattered rides never had. To me, he was just the sorrel gelding, his coat a shiny reddish brown color. He was new, he had no name, and he wasn't mine. My aunt and uncle allowed me to use him to try out for the princess position.

He was a lot of horse, and I will admit there were a few mishaps in the practice pen where he got away from me and tested my authority. Horses are aware of the weight and maturity of their rider. I was stick-thin and not into the idea of getting any "ranchier" than I had to. Slow and steady, *clippity clop* was my style of riding horses. Yet here I was, on a fancy horse, practicing princess routines in an ARENA.

I loved riding, but I didn't love *riding.* I enjoyed the connection with nature and peace that it gave me. The slow days moving cattle and the conversations on our walks home were my favorite. I was never your typical cowpoke, and the fast and furious life you see in old Western movies wasn't my thing.

I just loved being outside, clearing my head.

Instead of turning left for our figure eight, the horse went running full speed to the end of the arena, searching for the gate to escape with the other horses. Dad was in the barn waiting for me to finish up practicing. I pulled on the reins in fear, but he only went faster. When he finally realized there was no escape route, he calmed down so I could gather myself.

Dust whipped around us as the wind picked up, and the arena seemed even longer now that I was at the other end. The new horse and I sat there, waiting to see what the other one was going to do next.

His ears twitched.

"Asshole," I mumbled under my breath. A nine-year-old on the ranch only cussed when Mom and Dad weren't around to hear.

"Dad!" I shouted, my voice shaking as I made my way back to the barn. Dad was waiting for me at the entry to the arena, not alarmed by my nervousness. He was used to me freaking out.

"Don't put up with that shit. You're the boss." He stood next to my horse patting my leg. I still felt my nerves trembling down to my toes.

It took me a while to get over that day, but I continued to practice and eventually found myself in town, in an arena, trying out for Tiny Tot Princess.

I still wasn't fond of the idea.

I looked down at the purple shirt and dark blue jeans I'd picked. My boots peeked through the stirrups and I could see the shine Dad brushed on before we left the house. My aunt and uncle let me ride that fancy horse, and I wasn't used to it. His coat was as shiny as my boots, and I felt out of place. It felt like the difference between an old manual work pickup and a Ferrari. I would take 4-low any day over this bullshit.

I was uncomfortable with the arena. I saw more accidents in that small space than I ever did in open pasture. It didn't help that people were watching me ride. I wasn't one for audiences, and I'm still not. Little girls rode around, dudded up, prancing around. Their faces were full of joy while mine was full of anxiety and fear. I watched the other girls perform before me, noticing some of them even wore makeup. They also wore those blingy shirts I'd protested against when Mom took me shopping for the tryout. Why the hell was I here, again?

The scene wasn't my style, but my competitive nature still pushed me forward. I replayed the routine in my head. It was a simple figure eight interchanging between a trot and a gallop. The only part I was really worried about was talking to the judge. As the little girl before me rode out, Dad led me to the arena entry.

"I'm the boss. I'm the boss," I whispered as Dad opened the arena gate for me to complete my tryout pattern.

I went to another space, feeling like no one was there but me. The lope felt beautiful as I slowly floated through the figure eight. I saw the judge and knew it was my cue to stop.

"Whoa…" I said in a low, calm tone. Like magic, my horse put on the brakes. He put his butt to the ground, and though I probably didn't look like the famous horse riders on television, I sure felt like one. He tucked his head as I backed him up in front of the judge so she could ask me the princess questions. You know, cheesy questions like, "What does it mean to you to be a princess in this county?" and, "How would you represent the court for us if we chose you?"

Once we were done with the questioning, I took my glory run out of the arena and did my queenly wave to the nonexistent grandstand crowd. This time, the fake queenly wave didn't make me nauseous because I'd just nailed my routine.

We waited for the results, and to my surprise, the name they announced as Tiny Tot Princess wasn't mine.

"It was probably the questions. I never smile enough." I looked at my parents, trying not to show my disappointment. I don't think I really wanted to win Tiny Tot Princess, but hearing them announce another name sucked. I overcame a lot of fear to complete that tryout. I practiced so much at home, even when I was scared. Hell, I was riding a freaking young horse while doing it too. I felt like I'd just proved my horsemanship skills from the ranch. *That* is what hurt the most. Those skills weren't enough to be a princess.

Dad had lectured me before to never make excuses or say that the person who won didn't deserve it, so I left it at that. I knew that I probably wasn't as bubbly or as cheery as the other girls in their interviews. I had been told before in the county fair show ring that I was "too serious." Tears welled up in my eyes and I looked down at the ground, trying to hide it so my parents didn't think I was being a brat.

"You don't need to be a princess anyway. You're a real cowgirl," Dad grumbled as he loaded my horse into the trailer.

That was really the only statement I needed to feel validated. I never wanted to be a princess. But being a cowpoke on the ranch? That meant something.

There were times I wanted to go off on people when they visited the twins. There were times I wanted to march them into the NICU and show them the machines my kids were hooked up to. But that's one thing about where I come from: I don't need to prove shit to anyone. I was their mom, I was the boss, and I knew exactly what they needed.

The day I tried out for princess, I knew I wasn't their cup of tea, but no matter what, I was still Dad's cowpoke. I think in motherhood, all the negative comments and unsolicited advice can be so overwhelming. I remember sitting in my living room with comments flooding in, feeling like I would explode at any minute.

"Do it this way."

"Oh gosh, stop worrying so much."

"Never wake a sleeping baby."

"Your schedules are never going to work."

"You won't be able to keep up with breastfeeding for much longer."

The point of the princess tryout wasn't for me to win: it was for me to hold true to who I was. Having kids is similar, because there are a lot of opinions and ways people think you *should* be. You just can't please everyone. It's impossible.

You're going to piss people off, and you probably won't fit

into the perfect mold that you thought you would. Having twins who were born so early was a rare occurrence. When I realized that I knew more than the people trying to give me advice, I stopped doubting myself. I looked back to how scared I was to ride that two-year-old horse.

"Don't put up with that shit. You're the boss." Dad's words repeated in my head. I didn't need to please anyone. I was their mom, and I was the boss. I had to be brave for my kids and do what *I* knew was right, regardless of how everyone else felt.

CHAPTER THIRTEEN

THE BABY MONITOR STATIC WAS AUDIBLE JUST OUTSIDE THE opening of the shower. Josh and I sat in silence, letting the water run over our bodies. We'd made it ten months into parenthood. Once again, we found ourselves in the double shower, the place where the rawest of emotions always seemed to fester. Our hearts were full, but our mental stability was shaken. The warm water was soothing, and the droplets were the perfect way to unwind after a day in our lives.

We were doing it all. We'd both kept our careers and we spent equal time caring for our kids. We had no daycare charges, we both got to spend quality time with the boys, and the double income had us financially stable. From the outside, it looked like the perfect life. But we were crumbling.

Josh worked for twenty-four hours, and then he was home for forty-eight hours. Essentially, he was only gone every third day, which allowed him to be with the kids when I was at work and vice versa. One day out of the week, my sister or my mom watched the boys. Other than that single day, we were doing our best to spend as much time with our children as possible and keep excelling at both of our careers.

Josh broke the silence after ten minutes of staring at the wall. The next words that came out of his mouth needed to be said, but they were a huge turning point in our lives, even more so than the whole NICU stay. Our marriage was facing some of the biggest obstacles it ever faced. We were dealing with our own emotions, our own mental health, and enough time had passed since the boys were so fragile that everything was starting to come to the surface. We were not OK.

"I'm just so tired." He looked at me, trying to gain solidarity, I think. Instead, it made me lash out in anger.

"I don't care if you're tired, and I don't care if you feel over-whelmed! I taught from home when they were newborns! I still kept the house clean! I. DID. EVERYTHING!" I took the small comment and turned it into a huge fight—one that needed to happen.

"Why are we going tit for tat right now? I'm struggling working twenty-four hours at a time and taking care of the kids. I just need to vent." Hearing this sent me even further into unneeded rage.

"All we did was pray for them to come home, and all you do is complain now that they're here! If you can't handle it, then get out and I'll do it on my own!"

"Wow…" Josh looked at me, dumbfounded by the awful things I had just said to him. He got his towel, picked up the baby monitor, and left me alone with my thoughts.

"I hate you!" I had never spoken those words to anyone. They blurted out at Dad, out of my control, as I pointed my long skinny finger at both of my parents. I didn't really know what else to say. I was so frustrated that my parents were fighting. In the years between my sister and my brother's births, my parents had their ups and downs. The older I got, the more it hurt me to see them be so ugly to each other, especially in front of my little sister.

I screamed at both of them. My voice was strong in conviction as I lectured them about their fighting. I let my tears flow down my cheeks and the moisture ran down my neck, my pajama top the only thing stopping it. I was not ashamed of how I felt in my own home. My feelings were out there in the open, as they always were with my parents.

This was the first time I saw Dad cry. He sat at the edge of his bed, his tears matching mine. Mom's face was red from her amplified sobbing, and we all sat in silence, wiping away the tear streaks from our faces. The words that came out of my mouth had almost immediately ended whatever fight they were having.

"Come here," Dad said softly. He apologized for yelling, but I could tell that I hurt him. "Let's go watch something on TV while your mom showers." He led me into the living room, where I found a documentary I'd rented from the school library. I always enjoyed sharing my love of animals with both of my parents.

As I popped in the VHS tape, I didn't want to think about what had just happened. I don't think my parents did either. Scenes of a pregnant polar bear played on the boxy television set, which was propped on a small stand in the corner of the room. The seat kicked up when Dad pulled the lever on our sectional couch recliner. I leaned close to him and he scratched my head, something that always brought me comfort.

My sister must have fallen back to sleep after I left our bedroom. The house was quiet again. Sitting there in the middle of God's Country, the only ruckus was the ruckus that we made. Luckily, we were done with that for the night.

The thing is, I knew we were all going to be OK. There may have been bumps in my parents' marriage, but there was always love, grit, and loyalty too. The only thing we really had living in the middle of nowhere was each other, and letting arguments or hard times get in the middle of our family just wasn't an option.

They weren't perfect, and there's never an excuse for the way that they fought in front of me. They were fighting battles that I didn't understand at the time, but I definitely understand now. They were trying to raise kids in a messy world, grasping for their mental sanity.

As a little girl, I was so angry. As an adult with children, I feel validated.

This shit is hard.

———

As I sat in the shower alone, I remembered how awful I'd felt when I told Dad I hated him. I may as well have just told my husband that. The people that we feel the closest to in this world often get the brunt of our emotions because we feel so comfortable around them. Parenthood can lead to awful words and emotionally charged conversations.

I understood now that a lot of the fights my parents got into were caused by us, the kids. Do I think they ever blamed us? No. I do think it's obvious that being responsible for small humans puts an unexpected load onto any marriage.

Josh and I had just gotten done with a sixty-seven-day NICU stay. We were dealing with everyone in our face. Oh, and did I mention we had twins? The mental and physical demands the kids were putting on us were pushing us further than we could handle. Instead of taking it out on the precious humans we wanted home so badly, we took it out on each other.

Josh was at work full-time, dealing with the pandemic up close and personal. I only took eight weeks off after the boys came home, continuing to teach from home for the remainder of the school year.

When I went back to work, I think we both just went on

with life as usual even though it was anything but the usual. We were in a global pandemic, we had two new babies, and we were BOTH working. To this day, I am not sure how we survived, and I still don't think we realized what we were going through. Until I wrote this book, I forgot how crazy it was, how hard it was on us. Then I thought a little, and I think they call that trauma?

We all went through a degree of trauma during the pandemic, whether we admit it or not. Our world was—and still is—an unpredictable place, and it's definitely not the same world our parents grew up in. Parenting is tough right now, but the people that God chose to be parents during this time are even tougher.

We weren't giving ourselves grace, and we weren't addressing the pain we'd gone through. Before that fight, our marriage was on autopilot, and although hurtful words were said, I knew that we were going to be OK. Because love and faith will always persevere over charged emotions.

CHAPTER FOURTEEN

OCTOBER 2021

THE BELLS RANG, AND I CRINGED AT THE THOUGHT OF teaching the blood flow of the heart one more time. I'd missed work so much during the pandemic and while on maternity leave. I wanted to be back in a rhythm. I missed the structure, the kids, my coworkers—all the things that the last two years had deprived me of. Unfortunately, my return to school was not what I expected.

As I walked into the hall between passing periods, I felt like a stranger. This place had been my home for most of my adult life now, but now it was more like I worked in a prison. The students were the inmates, and we were the guards. Kids said hello to me, and I didn't know their names. They'd seen my face on screen all last year, but I rarely saw theirs. They knew my story, but I didn't know theirs.

I was still getting used to the fact that we had one-way hallways now. Kids were directed to walk this way, something that had been put in place to reduce COVID exposures over the past year. The mask mandates were still in place, and the social aspect I'd been hopeful to return to was not really social at all. Students fought us on wearing the masks, and staff referred to them as chin diapers because that was how most of the kids wore them. If we spent all day policing the masks, there was no room for doing the real job: teaching.

I did my best to teach the content each hour, but each hour I realized how much my kids were struggling, not only academically, but mentally. Some of my most productive days were the days that we got into groups, talked a little bit about content, and got to have conversations about how life was going. They needed human connection.

Each lecture period when I got to sit down and breathe for a while as the students worked independently, I did my best to keep up with my lessons. It was a time for me to reflect on what the kids needed and how to move forward.

"Mrs. Martin, I don't think I've learned anything in the last school year," a student said to me when they were getting help at my desk. I'd just finished repeating myself for the forty-five millionth time when they walked up with their heart diagram.

"I believe it." Unfortunately, they were right. I'm not sure if there was any learning going on or if we were all just trying to survive this crazy phenomenon. We were trying to teach kids while people were dying, political wars raged, and state and federal mandates were constantly changing. And yet there we were, trying to act like nothing had happened. *This is fine. Everything is fine.*

The part you'll love is that even as chaotic as this was, it still gave me the sense of structure that I craved. I'd been teaching online, then pregnant, then in the NICU, then teaching from home with the twins on oxygen, and back again. It was still chaotic, but it was getting me back to as "normal" as you could get.

Because of my teaching job, I had to be precise with my tasks. I had meals prepped, laundry days scheduled, and alarms set every day. There was a slight problem, though… Teaching wasn't teaching anymore. The pandemic was not just a virus, it was the

beginning of the fall in education. We were no longer teachers—
we were soldiers in a losing war.

My days were so mentally draining that I often came home
looking like a character from *The Walking Dead*. I found myself
falling asleep on the couch before our favorite television shows
even finished the intro songs. I was burning the candle from both
ends, and I wasn't sure how much longer I could continue on.

When I was at the school, I was giving every ounce of myself
to those kids. I was trying to close the gaps that had opened, I
was trying to control student behaviors to keep the school put
together, and I was trying to be supportive for my coworkers.
Every time I walked into that building, I knew there would be a
new challenge. Those challenges were no longer about teaching
content. I was healing these students from what they had gone
through, and all of us were trying to keep up with the demands. I
had up to thirty-five students in each hour-long class period.
Every day, the well-being of two hundred students weighed
on me.

Having twin boys had left no wiggle room for me and my
husband. We were either working, keeping up the house, or
sleeping. A job that had once brought me so much joy had
turned into just a job. Leaving my babies at home wasn't hard for
me because my husband watched them while I was gone, but my
mental capacity was running low.

What was I going to do now?

As we traveled down the dirt road, I looked back at the cloud of
dust that followed behind the gooseneck. I leaned on the door
staring at the rearview mirror, annoyed that we had to go back to
the CRP: the Conservation Reserve Program. Kylie was there that
day, and I put up my pretend plexiglass barrier between us so it
was almost as if her voice was muffled. I'd gotten really good at

zoning her out since she was born. It wasn't that I didn't like her; she just seriously exhausted me. She NEVER stopped talking.

My elbow rested on the window, and I watched the endless desert of God's Country pass by. It was picture frame after picture frame of brown landscape.

The CRP was a place of refuge for our cattle during the drought. We didn't have enough grass to feed our herds, so we took them elsewhere. It was a sad place, just like everything else was that year. God's Country was brittle, the land crunching beneath our feet. As we pulled up to the CRP, I saw that it wasn't much better. The fences were just strung-out, hot wire, and all I remember was there was So. Much. Dirt.

The task, yet again, was supposed to be easy, but as we know from everything else on the ranch, just because it is a simple task does not mean it will be easy. The horses backed out of the trailer: 202, Whitey, and Bay Mare.

Bay Mare stood at around sixteen hands high, bred from race horses. Dad hated her, but I loved her. She was beautiful in my eyes—big, tall, strong. I remember loping around on her like I was floating on a cloud, but I wasn't riding her today. At the ranch we had to horse hop to give each worker a break. I had graduated from the privilege of riding the oldest horses because my sister was the youngest. I was now riding Whitey, and Kylie was riding 202, the oldest, calmest horse we had. He used to be my comfort zone, but I no longer had that option.

Dad directed us to watch the gate so he could maneuver a rogue cow into the correct pen. I watched as he walked toward the herd and picked out the convict who had escaped. At that moment, I realized why he had chosen to ride Bay Mare. The escape artist we were chasing after was ONE BIG BITCH. I knew this was going to go south when Dad rode close to her and her nose tilted in the air like a prissy Valley girl who'd just stepped out of the Hilton. The prance that followed made me nervous. She was not scared of us. The body language she'd just presented was typical for unruly cows. She was definitely one of THEM.

The cattle were scattered around the water tank, a large tractor tire that was cut in half. Mud gathered around where cows splashed over the sides when getting in and out of the water. The water they drank was the same water they bathed and shit in. Lovely, I know. The sound of splashing amplified as Dad rode into the crowd of cattle. They all jumped out of the water, kicking up mud as they left.

Dad started to push her near the gate, and instead of running, she turned back around on him. She stopped in her tracks, almost like he'd offended her. I watched her, glancing at my sister, and scanned the rest of the pen, watching the gate like I was told.

As I stood in the opening of the gate, a bull inched slowly toward us. This was not what I needed right now. I was such a fearful cowpoke, and it unfortunately was because I had seen what these animals were capable of. I knew that I was going to have to put my big girl panties on and push him away while making sure my sister watched the gate behind me.

Damnit, damnit, damnit.

Whitey's ears pinned back. As the horse who loved working, I knew she had my back. The problem was that Whitey didn't need much direction, and I worried she would kick it into turbo and throw me off. In 2008, we were both around thirteen years old, and she was experienced and agile.

The bull bellowed and grumbled low moaning noises. He was a BIG SON OF A BITCH.

So now, not only were we dealing with a BIG BITCH, we were also dealing with a BIG SON OF A BITCH.

I looked up to see Dad in a literal battle with the cow. *Boom!* The cow charged at Dad's stirrups. Bay Mare stood her ground as the cow reared up for another blow. Dad took the honda, the hard part of a rope, and twirled it as the cow prepared to take another crack at Bay Mare.

You could hear the air moving as Dad wound up his rope. The propelling noise got louder and faster and—

Crack!

He cracked her on the face and she still didn't back down. The CRP made these cattle unruly, and I was not about it.

My sister and I sat in the gate, praying the burly bull stayed back. He continued to paw at the dirt, showing off in front of the ladies. I watched as Dad struggled, but we were told to watch the gate, and I wasn't really interested in helping him wrangle the cow.

The battle continued. She took a blow at Dad and he took one at her. She started to run, and I saw Dad situate his rope. He was done with her shit.

Thank God.

Both animals, the cow and Bay Mare, started sprinting. Bay Mare's long-legged stature caught the squatty cow in a few leaps. The rope flew through the air, and I prayed it landed.

A catch.

We always tried doing things the easy way, giving cattle the option to cooperate. Unfortunately, the cattle that get out are the ones that usually tend to be uncooperative.

She was slowly led by the rope out of the CRP pasture to where she needed to be. That was just the beginning of our day.

That year, although hard to understand as a child, I saw the hardships that we had no control over. The economy was at an all-time low, and so were our animals. There were no Christmas bonuses, and the plains of God's Country were barren. The good years seemed far from ever being possible again, but our family buckled down.

Perseverance isn't for the comfortable. It can only be accomplished by those who are OK with feeling uncomfortable for extended periods of time. Those few years on Rush Creek were probably some of our family's hardest years mentally and financially. I found comfort during the pandemic in knowing how to persevere.

I write this book not just to share these stories with you, but also to build solidarity. Though life can sometimes seem perfect through the screens of your devices, a lot of us are just persevering. The entire school year after we returned to "normal," we all were just surviving. I was figuring out how to be a working mom in a job that wasn't the dream career I signed up for.

I was slowly drowning in a quicksand type of scenario. We were just living in a Groundhog Day of chaos. I was thankful for the double income and the lack of serious daycare costs, but what about my mental health? So many people had convinced me that I was so lucky that everything worked out. I was able to keep my job, and we were full-time parents. But I was burnt out.

I knew that big changes were coming for me, but I wasn't exactly sure what. I knew that this type of life couldn't be sustained, but I was also in the middle of a school year.

As I sat in the classroom in October of 2021, I could no longer envision this being my home for the next thirty years. The thought of being the emotional support for my students, my coworkers, AND my family was inconceivable.

I'd brought my own kids into this world, and it was my responsibility to give my all to THEM. It was my responsibility to persevere through this situation and figure out the next plan of action.

I just had to determine what that plan was. In the meantime, I kept teaching.

CHAPTER FIFTEEN

DECEMBER 2021

WITH THE KIDS NAPPING, I HAD A MINUTE TO BREATHE. THE weekend allowed me a few hours of downtime, and I tried to recharge my battery. It seemed impossible to relax in my current situation. It was December in Colorado, and Christmas break neared. I went to work in the dark and I came home in the dark —the night that never ended. It made me anxious, manic in some ways. My mind raced, and I searched for what was missing. I found myself thinking about my current job. That school was my home. That was my family. How could I leave?

I typed into my Pinterest search bar…

How to make more money.

For some reason, I thought that money would solve my problems.

The values of the ranch were often centered around hard work and providing. I took on a lot of those masculine traits from spending so much time with my dad, our provider. It was my parents' job to put a roof over our head, keep us clothed, and put food on the table. I think my default attitude had always been to work hard and provide for those I cared for.

I changed my keywords in the search bar several times.

Passive income ideas.

Creative ways to make more income.

Ugh. Everything had to do with being social with other adults, or wouldn't allow me a flexible schedule with my kids. I scrolled and I scrolled until a pin caught my eye.

Have you ever thought of writing a book?

"Charming, great descriptions, and you really know how to entertain with your words." I skimmed the feedback before crumpling the creative writing assignment and throwing it in the dumpster as I walked to my three-hour chemistry lab. My 101 classes in college were a waste of my time, or at least I thought so. I had a really bad attitude, or maybe I was jaded from my science courses. My biology major drained me of life, and I no longer had the energy to care about a class that had nothing to do with my degree. I just wanted to make it out of there with my teaching license. That's it.

The following week, we had our final creative piece due. *Here we go again!* The best thing about science geeks was that everyone was an introvert like me, even the professors. Everyone was weird and had their quirks! They left you alone as long as you completed your work. These 101 classes were a mix of EVERY-ONE. They weren't specialized classes; they were the classes we were forced to take because, you know, college is extortion. My science peeps only spoke to you if you needed help. That was the way I liked it!

Every time I stepped foot in any of my elective courses, I cringed at the thought of all the extroverts that would be in the room. It was obvious that the ranch was a good place for me, with almost zero social interaction and plenty to do to keep my mind busy. I was definitely not on the ranch anymore.

My classmate finished reading his piece about going hunting

with his dad. We all clapped, and I admired the relationship he described with his dad. I didn't know many people who were from the sticks like I was. I was up next, and I cleared my throat. My double-spaced manuscript sat in front of me, and my palms became slightly sweaty. The paper dampened under my hands as I hit the desk with the small stack of my words. *Tap, tap, tap.*

Everyone waited patiently as I collected myself, and my story came off the pages. The easiest thing for me to write about was the ranch. It was, well, exciting. Some of the most sensory experiences I'd ever had happened there. It seemed embarrassing at the time to say, but the ranch was the coolest part of my life so far at eighteen years old. The rest of my life was just school, gaining academic accomplishments, and participating in all the same extracurriculars that all of my small town classmates did. It was pretty cookie cutter, so I chose something I thought these city kids would enjoy. What did I have to lose? I probably would never see them again after this class!

The particular story I read happens to be in this book. I wrote of the time that the cow tried to take on Dad and Bay Mare. I didn't include as many cuss words, but apparently I was funny? I'm not sure how, since I wasn't trying.

When I finished reading, I looked up, waiting for the applause to follow. There were smiles and nods as I looked around the room. I took a deep breath, thankful that my final project was over. I paused as I waited for my professor's feedback. *Just get it over with so I can sit and listen for the rest of class.*

"You know Kelcie, you should really consider writing a collection of short stories about your childhood! It was almost like I was there!" My professor smiled as he complimented me in front of the entire class. My face burned red, and I inwardly rolled my eyes. I didn't want to insult his compliment.

My professor looked like he was straight out of the nineties. His hair was long, stopping at his chin. And those jeans. He wore those Levi's that were a little washed out—you know the ones I'm talking about! I feel bad now for judging him. But the words I heard at home did cross my mind: "Damn hippie, he doesn't know what he's talking about!" But seriously, the hair? How was I supposed to take him seriously?

I clicked the Pinterest pin and soon realized that it wouldn't make me any money to write a book. (The amount of time and money that went into this project was pretty extensive.) I found myself in a nap time rabbit hole. I went from wanting to write a book to researching online colleges where I could get my PhD. Then I wrote down the pros and cons of being a stay-at-home mom.

What the hell was I doing? I didn't know what I wanted. Why was I looking at ways to make more money when we already made more than enough? It felt like I had these children that gave me so much happiness, but when they went to bed, there was nothing left for me. I was unfulfilled and trying to fill a void. Money, degrees, and dwelling at home weren't going to fix anything. But what would?

For so long, my identity was rooted in my career aspirations. Then I became someone's wife, and after that, I became someone's mother. I was in a whirlwind of identities, but none of them were Kelcie. They were all what someone else had labeled me.

I heard crying on the baby monitor and dragged myself out of the rabbit hole back into reality. Back to the grind.

My first Christmas break after returning from maternity leave was quickly approaching, and I thought maybe I would gain some clarity over my two-week break. I had a four-day trip to Paris planned with my best friend. Maybe that would give me the answers I wanted.

CHAPTER SIXTEEN

DECEMBER 2021

It was my first international trip away from the twins. I was going to meet my best friend Cortney and her Aunt Janie for their biennial trip to Paris. I was only going for four days, but it didn't matter. This was something I hadn't been able to do in the depths of motherhood, and I promised myself and Josh that I would never let that part of me go. I was yearning to explore somewhere new and hopefully gain some insight to my future.

My love of travel started in college when I traveled to Costa Rica on a conservation project for endangered sea turtles. That trip made visiting new places and learning new things an addiction. I found myself in Ireland, South Africa, Italy, and Mexico between the year I graduated college and the year the pandemic started.

Although I'd traveled before, I'd never experienced the airports around Christmas time. The noise was almost comforting. I didn't have my responsibilities with me. My kids weren't on my hip, and a diaper bag didn't weigh me down. I wasn't looking to my husband to see if he was OK. I was just part of the giant crowd. I liked it.

Social media comments rolled in, and I received texts about my trip. Everyone was so surprised I was only going for four days. Why even go? Little did they know that after the past two years, I needed this trip by myself, traveling across the ocean. I didn't care how long it was.

I hopped planes in New York, knowing that Paris, France was my next stop. The flight attendants gave me whatever I needed, and it felt so special. Someone was catering to me. The younger version of myself would have been so anxious to get there, but this new version of myself appreciated every part of the journey, not just the beautiful city waiting at the end of it.

When I landed, Cortney, Janie, and I hit the ground running.

I sipped my mulled wine, my breath fogging my view of my best friend and her aunt. We were in *Paris*. I pushed away the guilty thoughts about leaving my kids at home and looked at where I was. The streets were cobblestone, narrow in width. Everyone sat outside under heaters smoking their cigarettes, and I watched in awe at how different this world was, while mine was still continuing at home.

The waiter mentioned something to my best friend's aunt in French.

"He says you girls are very beautiful." She winked at us and smiled. Janie lived in France when she was younger, and she was one of the reasons we were there. She was once married to a French man, and her story was so…exciting. Every two years, she visited because she missed the food and some of the culture. Janie was in her seventies, but her spirit was still in her twenties; still a young woman in France.

Our trip consisted of wine, mulled wine, croissants, gourmet dinners, and more wine. We explored in the frosty month of December, visiting specific landmarks and admiring the Christmas trees that decorated the city. We laughed and toasted champagne at the cabaret, deciding if the women's boobs were real or implants. We giggled as we realized every man that we tried to hook my single best friend up with was gay. Hooking her up with *her* French husband was a complete fail.

I'd traveled to Europe before, but this time it was different. I did have my babies pulling at me from home, but I also had a sense of appreciation for being alone. I didn't get that time anymore as a mother. My last year had been consumed by surviving and trying not to lose my shit. Was I actually living again?

Down past my knobby knees, I stared at my scrunched toes. My long, narrow feet matched the rest of my scrawny limbs as I awkwardly stood at the bank of the creek, dressed in my white flowered panties and a matching undershirt. I fiddled with the tiny pink bow they always put on little girls' undergarments.

My parents stripped off their clothes and stepped into the water. I listened as my mom giggled, and I wasn't really interested in getting in. The bend in the creek reminded me of the islands I had seen on the television. The way it wrapped around the sandy embankment made me feel like I was at the ocean. The sun beat down on the small area, creating small glitter effects on the water. I started to imagine what may be lurking underneath the surface of those pretty specks…

"Come get in, babe. We'll hold you." Mom coaxed me with her hand.

I went with my dad instead, because naturally I always wanted to be with him. We waded in the cool creek water for a while. Dad took me to some shallow water to see the tiny bass babies swimming around. Seeing these cool little creatures calmed my nerves about what else could be in the water. I still wondered if the fish would bite my toes if we stood still too long. Although it looked like a beach, we weren't in clear blue waters.

What's funny about this memory is that I don't remember my

parents' skinny dipping. I don't remember it being weird or uncomfortable. I just remember how simple it was. There was no one around, and we were simply enjoying the moment.

I watched as Mom and Dad waded in the murky creek water. I had given it a try, but I was more interested in the tiny creatures Dad had pointed out earlier. The little bass were so small. I squatted next to the shallow water to watch them swim. The sound of the water and my parents' conversation comforted me.

Little did I know, that simple moment was spent in one of the most beautiful places I would ever see.

"I've been married, divorced, remarried... I was a teacher, I lived a lot of my younger years in France... The thing is, you'll figure it out. Whatever makes you happy, you'll figure it out. It's OK to change your mind or do different things within your lifetime!" Aunt Janie sipped her wine as she gave us these wise words.

Cortney and I were both in very different stages of our life, but we saw how the world could expect things from you and make you think that you had to follow a straight and narrow path. Cort had left her nursing program and completely changed her degree to be a speech pathologist. I was in my first year back teaching, and until this trip, I'd thought that was what I was going to do for the next thirty years.

As Cortney and I walked the streets of Paris, arm in arm, I felt like I'd stepped out of my routine at home. It was almost as if I had to remove myself from the mundane cycle to snap out of it. I'd just been surviving that whole time. I wasn't living.

The simplicity of the croissant and coffee every morning warmed my heart. The pieces, so buttery and light, dissolved quickly when I washed them down with the stout caffeine they called café. It reminded me that my moments were so precious; my alone time must be treasured. Back home, I had little things like croissants and coffee, but I didn't allow myself to enjoy them. I found myself drinking coffee while I cleaned, only to warm it up again in the microwave three times. There were times I put the boys down to nap, only to start folding clothes to "catch up." I wasn't unhappy with my life. I just didn't let myself enjoy it.

In Paris, no one knew me. There was no job, there was no home I had to take care of, no babies needing my attention… there were no responsibilities, except for myself. The boat for our tour approached the Eiffel Tower. I almost broke my neck to keep looking at it as we passed by. The wine never stopped flowing, and although it often made my head dizzy, I think it was giving me clarity.

My short stay in Paris was coming to a close, and I couldn't wait to get home. Christmas was only a few days away, and I was refreshed. I was ready to enjoy the holiday with my family.

As the airplane landed in Denver, I knew that I had those same simple moments at home. I was raised in God's Country, the most beautiful place in the world. Most of my favorite memories were based on simplicity, like skinny dipping. The laughter, the exploration, the act of sitting with your thoughts were all things I used to do on the ranch. I didn't remember how clean our home was, or how much my parents did at work. I just remembered my time with them. It didn't take anything extravagant to make me happy then, so why should it now?

I had simple things at home, I just had to figure out how to savor them. My kids were sucking the life out of me, and that was OK, but sometimes I too needed a break. I needed to leave the country to see that I was so blessed, but I was letting it pass me by because I didn't allow myself to find happiness in the little things.

I was wasting energy on drama that didn't matter at my job. I was finding household chores to do every second I had available. I spent my free time comparing my life to others, and consuming as much social media as I could. There could be hot coffee here, there could be iconic views here, but it was up to me to let the expectations go. I didn't need to move to France to turn my life around. I just needed to figure out how to slow my life down just enough so I could enjoy it.

Christmas came and went. There were a few gifts under the tree for me, and there were also some trinkets in my stocking. But the best gift I received was an idea. Santa, or maybe God Himself, snuck into the depths of my overthinking, wire-tangled brain.

I was going to do something great, and it would be for no one else but myself.

CHAPTER SEVENTEEN

Our silverware scraped against blue ceramic dinner plates. Elmo played in the background as Josh and I inhaled the last bits of our food. Both of our professions had created this inherent habit of wolfing down meals to survive. Firefighters tend to get interrupted by emergency calls, and teachers have limited time to eat between grading, emails, short lunch periods, and school activities. It was sort of a handy skill to have when it came to having twins. There was hardly time to sit down and enjoy a meal.

Once we finished, I opened the dishwasher. To my surprise, it was plum full of clean dishes from the night before. I stacked the dishware together, clanging and banging, almost throwing it into the cupboards.

"You couldn't unload the dishwasher?" My blood started to boil. How could I get everything done when I was home with the kids, but he couldn't?

"Yeah, well, not everyone can be as perfect as you, Kelcie!" *Ding, ding, ding!* The fight was on. Except this time, instead of giving me the chance to take my next shot, Josh blocked me unexpectedly. His next sentence was enough to stop us both in our tracks.

"I can't breathe in my mask, Kelcie."

"Wait, what?" My guard came down immediately, and I wasn't sure what we were talking about anymore. I stood with a stack of plates still in my arms, and they suddenly felt really heavy. Just seconds before, I could have thrown the whole stack across the backyard, and now I needed all of my strength to put them on the counter. My gaze didn't leave his as I waited for more explanation.

"I was at work, and when I put on my mask to go into a fire, I had a panic attack. I couldn't breathe." The fear in his eyes was similar to the day I flew in the helicopter. We both sat staring at each other, waiting for the other to continue.

It seemed as though both of our jobs were getting the best of us. Public servants were being worked to the bone, and unfortunately, that's what both of our careers were. Our mental health individually, and together as a couple, was at an all-time low.

Josh broke the silence. "Between work and being home with the kids all day, I literally don't feel like I'll survive, Kelcie!" My heart broke. I was so caught up in my own struggles of motherhood and teaching, I didn't even realize what was happening to my husband. We were both falling apart. The dishes didn't seem like a big deal anymore, and I hung my head in guilt as I finished cleaning the kitchen after dinner.

I thought about Aunt Janie's advice in Paris.

"It's OK to change your mind."

Josh was working twenty-four-hour shifts, and then he was coming home to twin toddlers. The house was a wreck. We were barely able to keep up with small things like the dishes and making ourselves meals. I know it's normal for parents to struggle those first couple of years, but I often disregarded the amount of heart and soul we both put into our careers.

It looked like I was going to have to make that big change a lot sooner than I thought, for my mental health *and* my husband's.

As the last dish clinked into the slots of the dishwasher, my stomach sloshed with the food I'd just scarfed. I wasn't very good at taking care of myself, but the thought of my husband hurting made my stomach ache.

Bath time, stories, and kisses good night were mechanical that evening. I thought back to the past few months as a couple —the good moments, the fights, and the stress. The boys smiled and giggled, I pretended to be happy and loving, but the truth is, I should have known. How could I pretend that we were OK?

When we weren't giving all our love and attention to our kids, we were giving it to our students and our patients. Josh was the captain of his crew, and I was in charge of close to two hundred students a day. The day-to-day tasks at home were robotic, just about getting to the next day.

My head hit the pillow with my phone in hand, and the phrase, "I can't breathe," would not leave my side. It lay next to me, breathing down my neck. He would need support as he went through the chain of command at his job to address the situation. He couldn't continue working in a high-stress environment if he couldn't breathe when going to save other people.

At the same time, I needed to figure out how to help us both. How could I ease his stress at home with the boys *and* do something that fulfilled me in my new role as a mother?

I turned away from Josh, using my phone as a way to disassociate from the situation. I saw an old classmate of mine marketing her business online, and it actually didn't seem like the same pyramid schemes I had seen in the past. She was coaching people—a life coach. I thought this was kind of odd, because I wasn't sure there was such a thing as life coaches. I did remember one thing about her: she could write.

I found her Instagram account and slid into her DMs.

I thought, *What if she could make me a famous author? I'd*

make a ton of money, my husband could quit his job, and I'd enjoy writing…What if…

"Hey Kristyn, I hope you are doing well, I was wondering if you had any experience in writing books? Also how have you been? I think I am having a late twenties crisis…LOL."

I waited for a response, already regretting my decision.

What the hell was I doing?

CHAPTER EIGHTEEN

FEBRUARY 2022

"Let's catch up?!" Kristyn messaged me back on Instagram the next day. I opened it during my lunch hour and spent my limited break time sitting with my thoughts.

The last time I'd seen Kristyn was in high school. The person I was now didn't even know the person I was in high school. We were both adults now, homeowners with big girl jobs and all that jazz. I think the last time we'd talked, she was describing how people at her college assumed that country folk rode to school on their tractors and didn't have a clue about what went on in the city. We both had interests in the arts but never really spoke of them in the small town we were raised in. Our main focus was keeping our noses to the grindstone, participating in sports, and figuring out a way to get out of there.

My fingers hovered over the keyboard on my phone for several minutes until my neighboring teacher walked in to warm up her food in the microwave. The ancient machine revved as I hurried to answer her DM.

"I can meet tonight at around 7 p.m."

I knew I wouldn't have a chance to text her back once my coworkers got started with the lunchtime venting. We were in the lull of winter. Nothing exciting was happening anymore at school. The only positives were that we didn't have to enforce masks anymore and our workload had decreased drastically since we no longer had to have separate lessons for students exposed to COVID. But still, it was February. The days were still long, and the drives to and from work were still dark.

"Guess who just tried to turn in late work from December?"

"Only one more month until spring break."

"Imagine if we got paid for all of the extra duties we have."

"Another assembly? How are we supposed to ever teach if we're constantly taking them out of class?!"

I know it sounds bad, but there was a sense of security with my colleagues where we could talk about what was on our minds. At the end of the day, they were the only ones who listened, and they were the only ones who completely understood. We supported each other.

I shoveled my food down so I could prepare sheep brains for the dissection the following hour. Only in a science room would we eat lunch unbothered by formaldehyde brain juice. The preservative took over the room, and everyone finished up their food.

"Sorry guys, I have to get these ready or I won't have time to finish the dissection before the assembly starts." I snapped the rubber gloves on as I plunged my hand into the murky liquid.

The bell rang and I finished up, locking the scalpels away as I went to the hallway to monitor students. The key ring got stuck in the back pocket of my jeans and I maneuvered it so it wouldn't fall out. My biggest fear was high school students running around with blades unsupervised.

That afternoon flew by. I raced around disposing of dissected brain tissue and preparing the fresh setups for the following classes. The assembly had me on high alert, making sure students sat where they were supposed to, scanning the sardine-packed bleachers. I didn't have time to address the anxiety that was bubbling up about meeting with a friend I hadn't spoken to in years.

When I got home, Josh was gone, so I asked my sister to help me get the boys ready for bed and clean up dinner. It was a mad dash. Mac 'n' cheese-covered faces giggled at us as we bathed the chubby toddlers. I was starting to get excited for the call, but I tried to stay present during our bedtime routine.

"Purple cat, purple cat, what do you see?" I read the Eric Carle book a little faster than usual, knowing the call was planned right at their bedtime.

"I see a red bird looking at me!" The boys giggled as my sister brushed their teeth for me.

"You better go, Kelc." Kylie looked up at me as she kissed the boys goodnight.

I looked down at my phone. 6:55 p.m.

"Shit. OK."

I opened the Zoom call with a minute to spare. The loading circle went round and round, and I realized that maybe this was going to be the answer to my problems. She was a life coach, right?

———

Mr. Crawford flipped the page for the challenge question of the week. I began scribbling in my notebook, pondering how to find the correct answer. Every week he gave us a new challenge, and every week he bought me a Wild Cherry Pepsi when I got the answer right. My parents didn't keep pop in the house, so when I had the opportunity to get one for free, it made my day.

"Don't answer it out loud!" He pointed at me, wanting to give the other students a chance to answer before I did. He gestured with his hand to bring my paper up to his desk.

After first grade, my parents decided to homeschool me, and I spent two years using the ranch as my personal classroom. In fourth grade, I asked to go back. My return to public school made it obvious that the education I'd received the past few years was advanced in some ways and behind in others. My parents' personal strengths in school stood out when I returned to the traditional classroom. My reading and math skills were through the roof, but there were certain things about public education I didn't understand. We had to learn how to dissect questions for state tests. There were prizes attached to everything. And the homework—there was a lot compared to when school was at home.

When I got the question right, Mr. Crawford didn't even have to ask. He walked back from the machine and left it on my desk, the condensation dripping down the bottle. I looked forward to drinking it during our work time.

There were positives and negatives about public school. When I was done with my homework, I got to read as much as I wanted. I exceeded my Accelerated Reader points way ahead of schedule, and it felt kind of fun to get rewarded for something I loved doing. When I was finished with my homeschool day I either worked outside with Dad or helped Mom with my siblings. It felt nice to relax a little.

After I finished my math, there was plenty of time to dive into a good book. The librarian started making me pick more challenging material because she said Junie B. Jones was too easy for someone at my reading level. I knew it made the other students mad when I got a Pepsi for almost every math challenge question, but I'd learned one lesson from Dad that I will never forget: Never lower yourself to be at the same level as everyone else.

Although I never lowered myself academically, I changed myself socially. I was a cowpoke on the ranch, and being home-schooled isolated me from interaction that most kids my age were exposed to. It's not like I had no contact with the outside world, but my visits with friends were quite spaced out living on Rush

Creek. I noticed other kids made fun of me for using bigger words. When you only talk to adults, you use different lingo than school-aged students do. I also wasn't playing any sports except summer softball, and my other physical activity happened on the ranch.

The hard part of school was fitting in, and I soon realized a lot of the things I learned at home got you judged in the public school system. I didn't know how to play house, I was very direct with my playmates, and I talked about my parents A LOT. When you're a kid, you truly just want to fit in. As time went on, I slowly started to lose the cowpoke in me, and I didn't even know it. I was trying to be like everyone else. I shouldn't be hard on myself about this time in my life because I was only a kid, and it's hard for me to look back on these days as "bad times." It wasn't all bad, but it was the beginning of losing myself, and that shakes me to my core. I think this happens to a lot of us, though. We realize that we don't fit in, so we try to mold ourselves into something everyone will like.

I finished my Wild Cherry Pepsi and the class lined up, ready to head to gym class. We were playing basketball that day, and everyone was really excited.

I would have rather kept reading.

The mousepad was wet from my clammy hands as I anticipated Kristyn's face on the screen. It took all of my mental power not to close the laptop in front of me. I sat in my bedroom, leaning against my headboard when she entered the Zoom meeting.

I instantly felt relief. It wasn't as scary as I thought it would be. I mean, come on—I'd known this girl since I was in fourth grade. Why was I so nervous to talk to her? Sometimes my social anxiety gets the best of me.

Although we were "catching up" as friends, we were also

having a discovery call, whatever that meant. There was some small talk—How have you been? How are things going?—and then a pause, the silence signifying that we were about to get into what this call was really about.

"So, you want to write a book?" Kristyn looked at me for confirmation.

"Umm, yeah…" I sat staring awkwardly at the screen.

"Do you know what you want it to be about?" Another question I didn't know the answer to. She continued to hammer me with questions, and when I heard them verbalized rather than in my head, I realized how lost I really was. I felt so overwhelmed, I was embarrassed to even be in the meeting.

"I just know I want to write a book." That was truly all I knew at the time.

"Well, it sounds like you have a lot of ideas, and you don't know where to start." She went on to explain what her rates were and what she really did as a life coach. She mentioned terms like limiting beliefs and having a clear intention of WHY you're doing something. Well, because I want to—duh!

I was trying to be polite, but I didn't understand why or how *I* would benefit from a life coach. I'd never had a problem accomplishing goals. I wanted to write a book, and *that* was what I needed help with. I wasn't really sure what all of the other questions were for.

I also felt embarrassed by the idea of paying someone to help me with my life. How pathetic was I?

"OK, well either way, it was good to catch up. Let me know what you decide!"

"Will do!" I replied as I exited the Zoom call.

That night, my mind raced as I thought back to how much every experience in my life had changed me—how much society had changed me. When I went back to public school, I slowly but surely did everything I could to fit in. Over time, I had completely lost the little girl I was on the ranch. That little girl was so sure of who she was and explored the world without hesitation. Now, I was sitting in my bed, interviewing someone to be my freaking life coach.

I had no clue who I was anymore, and it wasn't something I could blame on my kids. It was my own fault. I was so caught up in what I *should* be doing that I'd forgotten what I *wanted* to do.

I needed help, and I needed the humility to allow it.

The next morning when I woke up, I texted Kristyn.

"Sign me up."

CHAPTER NINETEEN

FEBRUARY 2022

I TRIED TO GET PAST HOW AWKWARD "LIFE COACHING" sounded. Seriously, was I a loser for needing someone to coach me through life? But we hit the ground running in our first session, and Kristyn definitely wasn't holding back.

"Do you enjoy your job?" Kristyn asked.

"I mean, yeah…"

I guess I just thought we were going to write a book, get it accomplished, and move on. She was asking me simple questions about my life that I found very uncomfortable. She wasn't asking hard questions, she was just asking all the *right* ones.

"What do you do for fun?" she asked next.

I stared into the camera on the Zoom call. I did this a lot in the very beginning. I seriously had no idea what I even liked to do anymore. I couldn't remember the last thing I did for "fun." If there wasn't money, accomplishments, or rewards attached, I wasn't doing it.

"Kelcie, there isn't a right or wrong answer to these questions! We're just trying to figure out what's going on." Kristyn looked at me with compassion. She could tell I was starting to get anxious.

I was beginning to wonder how I was functioning in my

normal day-to-day life. I felt like I didn't even have a personality anymore, especially when every question she asked was another one I couldn't answer.

Our first session ended with homework. All of the exercises were designed to make you think a little deeper and figure out what the real problem was. Throughout the week I wrote, hashing out all of the deep questions she was asking.

Write down what you like about your current career.

Write down what you don't like.

What activities do you consider your hobbies?

Writing it all on paper put things in perspective for me. There were hardly any things I liked about the current state of my career. I wrote down more negatives instead—burnout, correcting student behavior, no more room for advancement, the student-to-teacher ratio. It was all negative.

When it came to hobbies, I didn't have any. The only thing I did was watch Netflix, and even then I was so tired at the end of the day I couldn't make it through an episode. Every week that I did these homework exercises, I realized I was lying to myself.

It wasn't a question of what the problem was. It was a question of who.

I braced myself, covering my chest with my arms as the herd of girls ran down the basketball court. The ball handler had her eyes focused on the prize, ignoring my stance blocking the basket. She put her head down, ready for the and-1, looking for the shot and the extra free throw point. I closed my eyes, knowing we would soon be on the ground. I sat there praying that I fell correctly. In typical Kelcie fashion, I already had four fouls in the game, and I was about to get kicked out of the regional tournament. It would be my first high school appearance at state if we won.

I sat on my ass and looked up at the ref.

An aggressive hand to the back of his head with the other pointing toward our basket signaled an offensive foul. She fouled me; I didn't foul her. I did it. I changed the momentum of the game.

The crowd roared as my teammates helped me off the floor.

Most people don't know I was embarrassed by how terrible I thought I was at sports. I didn't start in kindergarten like all of my friends. The amount of natural talent I had was minimal, and I made up for it with brute force and ignorance. One of my teachers once compared me to Dennis Rodman. I later watched a documentary on the Bulls and I understood why. I was reckless because that was my only way to fit in and be part of the team. I contributed to the team by sacrificing my body, slamming into people, stealing the ball, and doing all the things that didn't require much skill, only tenacity. I was never a high scorer. My highest stats were often my fouls.

The tables were turning in the fourth quarter as my team-mates hit three-pointers. I shoved the tallest girls as we went for rebounds. I was one of the biggest girls on the team at five foot seven and 140 pounds. During my high school years, most of the teams had at least one six-foot girl, and some teams had two. I wasn't that big comparatively, but I was wiry.

We pulled away with around an eight-point lead, and soon we found ourselves qualified for the state tournament, thanks to my sacrifice that day.

Though everyone cheered for me, none of them knew my heart wasn't in it. I excelled as much as I could as a three-sport athlete, but I never had the guts to tell any of my teammates and coaches it was all a lie. I didn't really care if we lost, and I didn't really care if we won. I was more into the book I was reading at home, the latest craze on television, or my academic endeavors. I knew that I would do big things one day, and I had a feeling those things wouldn't involve sports.

The sad part about going to public school and participating

in organized sports was I often thought there were better things to do. I tried to believe that I was passionate about those activities, but they were someone else's dream. When you come from a small town, there aren't very many options for finding what you really like. At my school, you either played sports, or you were kind of an outcast. I didn't like being an outcast, so I continued to take part in the activities that helped me fit in.

Working through the life coaching exercises with Kristyn had me distraught. Looking back on my high school days made it clear: I was the problem!

When I left my hometown, I powered through my bachelor's degree and two master's degrees with remarkable speed. These were great accomplishments, but I didn't enjoy them. The career was nice, and the money supported my growing family, but that was the extent of it. When had I lost the creative, exploring little cowpoke I'd once been?

I was caught up in the rat race, the hustle culture, the get-ahead-and-compete-with-the-world type of lifestyle. I was good at it too. My ability to check off life milestones was out-of-this-world impressive. Writing a book in record time was just another attempt to check something off the list in hopes of feeling fulfilled.

I was uncomfortable sitting still with myself. I chased other people's ideas of what *should* make me happy, and I cried.

Truthfully, I cried after almost every session with Kristyn. I would sacrifice anything for anyone. I would work myself to the bone for my family and my friends, even my teammates, but what would I do for myself?

I couldn't answer that question.

Everything I was doing in my life, I was doing because I thought it was what I was *supposed* to do. I got married, I got a job, I built a house, I had babies. Shouldn't we all live happily ever after now?

I knew I needed to make this journey when I asked myself how my kids would remember me when I died.

I wanted them to see a woman who went after what she wanted in life. I wanted them to see their mom thrive and be proud. I didn't want them to see a woman who only lived to please others. What kind of example is that? We need children to know that it's safe to follow their dreams and take risks.

My babies changed my life forever in many ways. They made me realize life is too short to keep conforming. I was ready to face my demons head-on and be a role model. I would no longer be the person everyone counted on to maintain the status quo.

There were twelve sessions in my life coaching program, and what I thought would be a waste of time became a writing journey. I started a blog as a continuing creative outlet for myself. I began to build confidence and gain an audience on my social media platforms. I was exploring new outlets, educating myself on things I didn't have to. I was writing for fun rather than for a grade. I was doing it all for the joy it gave me. Everything was easier when I wasn't focusing on the end goal anymore. I was no longer sacrificing everything for everyone else. I wasn't taking the hits anymore.

I was going after *my* passions instead of everyone else's.

CHAPTER TWENTY

I WAS ONE SEMESTER AWAY FROM COMPLETING MY DEGREE and obtaining my teaching license. All I had left was to teach under a veteran teacher while they gave me feedback. There was one small problem, though.

When I showed up in January 2017 to complete my student teaching, no one was there. My principal had been surprised by a teacher leaving after Christmas break. That person who was supposed to be my mentor had dipped out, and there was now a science teacher vacancy. I sat in a classroom full of fifteen-to-eighteen-year-olds, terrified.

Science degrees are hard. I'd learned that in the previous three years of chemistry and biology courses. Judging by the amount of caffeine, tears, and mental breakdowns it took to get me to that point, it was arguably in the top five hardest things I've ever done in my life. Because no one else is as crazy as I am, there were no other science teachers available midyear to fill the position. I was their only option.

I was a twenty-two-year-old rookie, staring into the eyes of bloodthirsty high schoolers. I was the zebra, and they were the lions. Nothing like trial by fire, right?! I was speaking with every person in the school to try and convince them to let me teach under a long-term substitute position. I was depending on Josh at the time to pay our bills while I held down my work-study job at the college. We were engaged and really diving into what it would be like to be married supporting each other. I was only able to work Fridays, when I wasn't student teaching. I knew I could either work all week for free and work myself to the bone every weekend to survive the semester, or I could prove myself as a capable teacher.

Two veteran teachers rallied around me, and I stood my ground and held high expectations for my students. There was a reason the teacher before me wasn't there anymore, and it was my turn to give the students the education they deserved. I set rigid deadlines, and I encouraged class participation. I didn't give busy work, and I made sure students had to comprehend the material in my science class, not just breeze by. I came home every night exhausted. Nothing in my teaching program had prepared me for that! When I thought I would be writing lesson plans, I was just trying to keep my head above water. I was determined to prove myself.

After my first couple of weeks doggy paddling through lessons, I was called into the principal's office. I was prepared for him to tell me they were going to move me to another school while they found a substitute for the class. I wasn't technically licensed yet, and I knew that was a possibility.

"Go to the admin office and get your substitute license figured out, and we'll take it week by week," the principal directed me.

I jumped in my car, drove to the administration building, and darted inside. I was going to get paid. Probably a small amount, but I was going to get PAID.

When I got in my car, I was ready to sign papers agreeing to $100 a day. I was not complaining. That was way better than the $0 a day they were offering me to student teach. To my surprise, the HR lady handed me a salary contract with benefits included. This wasn't just a sub job, this was a BIG GIRL job. I thought she had me confused with someone else. She explained it would be easier to just hire me than to deal with a slew of subs for a whole semester. They helped me apply for an emergency license in the state of Colorado, and I was now a full-time employee at the local high school.

The January air was chilly as I ran to my car from the administration building. I scanned the parking lot before closing the door and warming up my Ford Taurus. I covered my legs with a blanket, rested my head on the steering wheel, and cried. My old janky car hummed as I screamed with excitement. My heater blew cold air. My teeth chattered, the amount of pride I had in that moment so unbearable that I wept there in the parking lot for ten minutes straight.

Just two weeks before, I'd been told I would be making no money to teach for someone else for the next few months. The struggles, the late nights studying, holding down three jobs—it was all worth it. There were so many times I wanted to quit, and as I sat in my car crying, I knew there was a reason why I didn't.

Once I collected my thoughts, the first person I called was Josh.

"Babe, I have a career now."

April 2022

The alarm on my phone went off, chiming every nine minutes. I hit snooze for the last time. If I didn't get up now, I wouldn't have time to shower before I went into work. I could hear the twins stirring in their cribs.

I rubbed the crust out of my eyes to see another notification from Indeed with more job opportunities. Ever since I'd started working with Kristyn, I had been on the job hunt. After six weeks of really hard work answering questions, I decided to continue writing on my personal blog. I also decided that my husband and I needed a change, and we were both trying to figure out how to alter our careers to put our family first.

Two months passed, and the application process was pretty disappointing. I could easily go teach at another brick-and-mortar school, but I needed less stimulation throughout the day. Since COVID, there were a lot more online schools hiring. For some families, it seemed to be a better fit. I thought that maybe if I was home with Josh on his days off, there would be less stress on him. After all, two against the twins was a lot better than taking them on by yourself. It also would leave more mental space for my writing. I noticed that the stories I was sharing with my small group of followers were healing. I was figuring out who I wanted to be, and guess what? I had a hobby—an *actual* hobby, not just watching half a Netflix episode and falling asleep. If I could work from home, it could change the course of the future for me and my family.

I scrolled through the job listings, annoyed. I told myself I was going to stop applying! I was burnt out. I was done. The end of the school year was approaching, and if I didn't find a remote job soon, I was going to give up looking.

There was one remote job in the three listings included in the email. I slammed my phone back on my nightstand. My body would not move. I looked over at Josh, still asleep. I imagined not having to get up so early every day to get ready and rush out of the house. The thought of having our morning coffee together on his days off sounded appealing.

GET IN THE SHOWER.

At this point in the school year, I had to mentally coax myself out of bed. There was an urge to burn all of my PTO and never go back. I. Was. So. Tired. As I showered, the water woke up my lifeless body, and I thought of the job listings. The remote position was the first one I had seen in a few weeks. Maybe this school would actually call me back.

I wrapped a towel around myself, threw a towel turban on my head, and sat on the toilet, contemplating my entire life. I still wasn't awake. I dabbed concealer under my eyes, threw my hair in a bun, and sifted through my stack of green staff shirts.

Maybe after the summer I'll be OK. Maybe it's just my first year back that's making things so hard. I kept trying to weasel my way out of the real issues, knowing damn well the school wasn't going to magically become normal after the summer. I needed to do this for my family, and I wanted to pursue being an author. I couldn't do that at the rate I was functioning.

Before I left the house, I uploaded my information to the job application. I had filled out so many at this point that it was all ready to go. I threw my phone back in my purse, filled my tumbler with coffee, and took a long drag. Coffee—elixir of life, healer of my soul—was the only thing that got me ready to drive to school.

The morning was a whirlwind; back-to-back classes flew by, projects scattered the room, and my colleagues buzzed all through lunch. Finally, my prep hour arrived and I was thankfully not subbing for another teacher's class. A stack of anatomy quizzes on the endocrine system sat in front of me. I sighed, finally getting a breather from my students and from my children. This was one of the very few hours of the day when some type of child wasn't in need of my full attention.

My phone lay buzzing beside my ungraded papers, and I jumped when I saw the name of the district I'd applied for that morning.

I cleared my throat, answering the phone with angst.

"Can we do a virtual interview tomorrow?"

This was it. I was getting my chance, just a month before summer started.

I'd gone through so much to get my current job. It was

disheartening to think of leaving it all. I loved teaching; I got into it to inspire kids, help them succeed. Along the way I saw students flourish, and I became a role model to a lot of them. My coworkers were my best friends, and I was trying not to cancel my interview all together.

This internal battle had been raging for the past few months, but the thought of sustaining my sanity over the course of thirty years in that classroom was my breaking point. I knew that with twin boys, there was no way I could continue to fight the mental fatigue that the school was causing me.

The following day dragged on, and all I could think about was the interview. It was hard for me to speak to my students knowing that if I got this position, I would be saying goodbye soon. I left as soon as the bell rang. The end of the school day was here, and the interview that could change my life was in thirty minutes.

I rushed home to set up my computer for my virtual interview. Josh took the kids to the opposite side of the house, distracting them so I could sneak away into a quiet place in our bedroom. Once again, I sat in front of a computer, clammy hands, watching the circle go round and round.

This was it.

CHAPTER TWENTY-ONE

THE DAY AFTER MY INTERVIEW, I FELT LIKE I WAS CHEATING on my current job. It was like I'd been in a five-year relationship and decided to step out on them after we had been through so much together. I knew the interview went well, but the anticipation was killing me. I kept thinking I could feel my phone buzzing in my pocket, only to reach for it and not see a single notification. I interviewed on a Tuesday and they promised an answer by Friday.

When I got home, it was all I could talk about.

"What if I didn't get it, Josh? What then? We can't continue on like this anymore. You're too invested in your job to leave right now. But what if you left? That would be fine too; we would figure it out. Right?" Our current life situation had me back to my oldest-daughter-fix-everything-handle-it-by-myself mode.

"Honey, you're going to get the job. First of all, I know you were the best candidate, but second of all, you know how hard it is to find science teachers. How could you not get it?" Josh tried to reassure me, but again, I always went to the worst-case scenario.

"You don't understand, Josh! I'm worried about you!" My voice raised, drawing his full attention from the dinner he was making. Olive oil popped as he added the leftover pasta to the cast iron.

There were no words for a while, only the sound of frying spaghetti. The leftovers saved us from having to cook, since once again we were ragged with exhaustion.

After the incident with Josh's mask, he'd contacted the higher officers of the fire department and made them aware of the issue at hand. If he couldn't breathe, he was a danger to himself, his crew, and the victims he was saving from fires. Most importantly, he was falling apart in his home, the one place he was supposed to feel safe.

"Josh, I've got your back."

He didn't answer me. I knew he felt ashamed that he was struggling so much with his anxiety at work. He was getting help in therapy and had been diagnosed with PTSD. The twins' traumatic entrance into the world, along with the pandemic and the high levels of stress at home, brought up a lot of feelings. He was coming up on fifteen years in the fire department. Since he was twenty-one years old, he had seen death, drug abuse, child abuse, and the darkest parts of the city we lived in. The demons that lurked all came forward when he was vulnerable. I couldn't see him this way.

Silverware clanked and our noodles slurped.

I had to save him. Getting this job was the only way I knew how. I needed to be home for him.

The first child we had together was our black lab, Mattie girl. I watched as Josh threw her bumper toy into the reservoir. The splash that followed was a cannon ball. There were no swan dives in her excitement.

It was the last day of summer 2017 before I started my first official year of teaching under my professional license. The previous spring semester—the chaotic one—I don't really like to count. Now that all of that was over, I felt like my life with Josh was really beginning. We were engaged, living together, and enjoying every bit of it.

The summer air was calm, and it felt like everything in the world was just perfect. Jet skis zoomed past in the deeper water. Families gathered in other small coves next to us, enjoying the reservoir just as we were.

The area was buzzing, but it was a normal buzzing. Kids played, snacks were dispersed. The lake was full of boats and other fun toys that adults like to spend their hard-earned money on. But suddenly, something broke the friendly buzzing.

It was a loud crack.

Then screaming.

Josh went running past me, emptying his pockets onto the dirt. I grabbed Mattie by the collar, unsure of what else to do.

I followed Josh, picking up his trail of belongings. Along the way he'd lost his tennis shoes, his keys, and his wallet. Before I could get everything picked up, he was in the water. A man floated right next to a jet ski, his body limp.

A pregnant woman stood screaming at the edge of the water, her other children hovering around her. I quickly put Mattie inside the pickup and ran to calm the woman down. I was so frozen with fear and panic, I didn't know what else to do other than try to soothe the situation.

I watched in awe. I knew Josh the fiancé. I didn't know Josh the firefighter. His water rescue skills kicked in immediately as he scissor kicked his way to the shore dragging the body. He had his arms under the man's armpits, holding his head above the water.

The closer he got to the shore, the more blood I could see. There was a laceration that started at the top of the man's forehead and exposed all of the flesh down to his eyebrow. The skin draped over his eye, blocking his vision on the left side.

The hysterical woman was already on the phone with 911, and I scanned the reservoir to assess the damage. A little girl popped out of the tall grass on the other side of the cove.

"Was she riding with him?!" I realized there were tears coming down my face. I had been sitting there crying in all of the action. Now I was freaking out again, because no one mentioned that he wasn't alone on the jet ski. I ran to the other side to check on her, and she looked at me, way too nonchalant for someone who was just launched across the water.

"I flew off." The little girl was unscathed. *How?* Also, how did everyone forget she was on the jet ski?!

As I brought her over to her mom, Josh was speaking broken Spanish. The man who was hurt didn't speak any English. I felt like I was engaged to a stranger, because I'd never seen this side of him. It was strange and impressive how quickly he became someone else.

Two jet skis had crossed paths. When they collided, the man and his daughter ran over the other rider. He was knocked unconscious and suffered a head wound. The ambulance showed up, and Josh handed off care to them.

"We'll let you know how his blood work comes back," the paramedic, who knew Josh, explained.

"Why do you have to hear about his blood work?" I asked, concerned.

"Because his blood got all over me, and I wasn't wearing gloves," Josh replied. I didn't realize how much first responders put their life and their well-being at risk every day. I also didn't realize how it flipped like a switch for them. While I was crying and running around like a chicken with my head cut off, he was saving lives.

After dinner and bedtime, we got into the shower. I was hoping to talk to him a little more about what was going on in therapy. I knew they were working on some deep stuff, but I often made matters worse with my constant worry.

"I just want you to get better, hun. I just want to fix it for you." I washed my hair, waiting for a reply. I half expected him to change the subject.

"You know what we worked on today? I had to describe a feeling I had in my body. I had to give my anxiety a physical feeling outside of my brain." He looked at me, pausing, waiting for my approval to continue.

"OK…" I coaxed him to go on.

"I can physically feel the weight of lifeless babies that I've held on some of my worst calls." He held out his arms like someone was about to load his them with firewood.

"When I hold the boys, I can picture those dead babies, and it feels like I can't move." As he talked, he wasn't talking to me. He was in the memories—all of them. He was there on the calls and he was there when we first held our boys. He was there with the oxygen tanks, anxious that they would stop breathing on his watch.

Suddenly, I was there too.

"I got my paperwork approved, and I'm going to be off work for a couple of months." He quickly changed the subject when he saw my tears welling up.

Josh kept the darkness away from me as much as he could. But he had held it in too long. There was no more hiding from these demons. We had to face them together now.

The job hunt started as a way to make myself happier, but it manifested into much more than that. I was looking for a way to save myself *and* my husband. We were both struggling, and we had two little boys that needed us.

I got the job offer that Friday afternoon. They matched my

pay, they offered me a fully remote position, and they changed the course of the future for me and my family.

CHAPTER TWENTY-TWO

THE NEW WORK COMPUTER BLINKED, READY FOR THE FIRST day of school. It was a strange morning. There was no rush to get out of bed, no searching for an outfit to wear, and no worries about traffic as I left the house. Instead of a to-go tumbler, I drank my coffee out of a ceramic mug and watched my kids run around the house while I geared up for my first work meeting.

We'd spent the summer enjoying our time together. Josh was off work for a couple of months, still continuing his therapy. It took a lot of work as a couple to get through it, but the break was exactly what we needed to restart. He had taken on fewer responsibilities at work since returning to the floor, and he had techniques to help him with his anxiety on the job. The tension released from his shoulders, his face relaxed, and the demons we were fighting a few months ago seemed to hide away for the time being.

The first meeting started and I was introduced to the new staff. We would see each other in-person in a few days, but this would be how the majority of our gatherings happened. They would be virtual. It was unreal to me that this was my new normal. There were no bells ringing, no students misbehaving, and no worried thoughts about my husband being at home alone with the kids all day. It felt like we were going to be OK.

The meetings rolled on. Learning platforms, communication platforms, and school policies were being thrown at me left and right. This had been my biggest fear of leaving my old job. I was starting over.

The sound of crackling bacon brought me right back to the reason I'd made this change. I was home. Breakfast was cooking, and I was able to eat at my leisure. I was no longer responsible for paying the mental tax to the brick-and-mortar every day. I was free.

My first day passed, and that turned into my first week. Before I knew it, we were a few weeks into school. Things were moving smoothly. I was overwhelmed by the new information, but I knew that with time, I would get into a rhythm again.

As the days passed, I couldn't help but realize I wasn't really writing that much. There was an occasional blog post here and there, but every time I sat down to start my book, I quit. I literally quit before I could even start.

The summer was spent figuring out how to get our minds well again, and the beginning of the school year was full of new information and exciting new growth in my career.

Now, it was time to write.

The Kiowa County Fairgrounds were lined with trailers. Kids rode their horses all over the parking lot, and I could see some of my fellow first grade classmates. Families parked their pickups and walked across the road to get ready for the gymkhana, where cowgirls and cowboys raced against the clock to show off their skills. This went against everything in my cowpoke conduct. I hated going fast on the ranch, so why in the hell would I want to do it here!? I left the speed demon work to Dad out on Rush Creek.

Dad never allowed me to ride around aimlessly. I was only allowed in the arena to warm up, never to "jack around." I obeyed those rules because I saw the accidents that can happen when you bring horses into town. It was a different vibe than cowpokin' on the ranch.

The air smelled of burnt nacho cheese and funnel cakes. Spectators filled the grandstands. The announcer stand played country music as the contestants warmed up. I. Was. So. Nervous. My dad wasn't there with me if something went wrong. He was out of town for a hunting trip. I didn't feel comfortable riding in an arena. I wasn't at home! I walked my horse out of the arena to my aunt and Grammy. Grammy knew I was nervous. She could always tell how I felt.

"Remember, slow and steady wins the race. You run your race, not everyone else's," Grammy whispered in my ear. That was exactly what I was going to do. Up until that point, I was embarrassed. I knew I wouldn't go as fast as all the other girls. I was afraid to. A lot of my fear came with the reality of what can happen when you go fast. Riding a horse is a risk every time you get on. No matter how tame the horse is, anything can happen. I'd seen kids thrown off, stomped on, and hanging on for dear life with no feet in their stirrups. Dad told me stories of people he knew getting caught in their reins and dragged to death. Horses are powerful beasts that a lot of people don't respect. I always chose to respect them.

That day, I took Grammy's advice and I ran my own race. I started with pole bending and barrel racing and I performed the patterns perfectly. I kept 202, my seasoned sorrel gelding, in a trot, sometimes shifting gears into a slow gallop. I watched the other girls my age complete the same patterns, emulating *The Fast and the Furious* movies. Along with that fury, there were mistakes. Contestant after contestant knocked down poles and barrels, and they were penalized. I gained confidence. Grammy was right. I was going to do it my way, slow and steady. I rode so slow in the goat tying event that the goat didn't even budge. Other girls ran so fast the goat tugged at the end of his pegged rope in fear. The flag race came. I rode to the first barrel, came to a compleeeete stop, grabbed the flag, and then slowly trotted to the next barrel to drop the flag in the opposite barrel. Again, I watched as the others ran past the barrel, ran around the barrel, and even dropped the flag! I felt even more confident. Although I was slow, I completed every event perfectly.

I knew I probably didn't even place in the top three of any of the events. I just felt happy that I carried myself with such confidence and ease. Slow and steady was who I was!

I took my horse to the trailer, where my family congratulated me. I couldn't wait to debrief with Dad about this when he got home. It would be a dinner conversation we'd both enjoy. Then the announcer started to announce the winners of the events. I placed in every single one! I didn't have any first place announcements, but I was happy with my consistency. Then I was asked to come to the announcer stand to get my winnings. I climbed up the stairs, jingling my spurs with each step. I remember feeling like I was so cool, because that's how Dad sounded when he walked too. When I arrived at the announcer stand, the prize that stood out to me in the woman's bag of awards was a big, shiny belt buckle. It gleamed in her hand and I looked at her in disbelief.

"We decided that you were our all-around cowgirl of the gymkhana today, Kelcie!" The announcer handed me my buckle and I grinned from ear to ear.

I was so proud of what I'd accomplished. That award still means a lot to me because I realized that day that I was a cowpoke. I was no rodeo girl. When I was true to myself and who I was, I succeeded. I still look back and remember that I didn't have anything to prove. I liked to move slowly, and I worked many days on the ranch. I didn't have to go fast or be somebody I wasn't. I knew who I was and where I came from.

Dad entered me into gymkhanas to push me out of my comfort zone and get me to try new things. I didn't thoroughly enjoy competing in those events, but I did learn something about myself. In my adult life, I realize that I have to explore the world and try things that make me uncomfortable. It's OK if I don't enjoy every single thing I try. It's OK if I'm better at some things than others. These life experiences helped me discover valuable information. The day that I won the all-around cowgirl buckle was significant because I learned that being slow and steady wasn't always a weakness. I learned that it was something that made me unique. I learned that finding your true self, rather than trying to be something that you aren't, will help you discover so many new things in life.

When I decided to start my book, I really had to find that slow and steady cowpoke who won all-around cowgirl. I dove headfirst into drafting, but it wasn't pretty that's for sure! I started writing this memoir at least six times between August and October of 2022. I wasn't used to writing such a large overarching story. I got discouraged many times, but I continued to write on my blog, create social media content, and do all of the research that I could.

I found a lot of authors I looked up to on social media who were paving the way in self-publishing. It was hard not to feel jealous of some of them. They were pumping out books at the speed of lightning. I couldn't even get the first chapter written.

But at the rodeo that day, I succeeded when I took it one event at a time, one barrel at a time, one pole at a time. I prospered when I stayed consistent.

I knew I had to keep the same mindset in this writing journey, or I was never going to make it through.

Slow and steady wins the race.

CHAPTER TWENTY-THREE

I turned the wheel opposite of the way expected, craning my neck behind me to see the gooseneck trailer. Dad was out of town, and the goats had been found fifteen miles north at the neighbor's house. Mom sat in the passenger seat, staring as her daughter prepared the trailer for our next adventure. She was an educated woman, but she wasn't so great in the "ranchy" aspects of our lives. Lord help us.

It was never my idea to get three hundred goats. Never. It was Mom's idea. She watched a movie in which a woman and her children had a successful sheep business. Of course Dad supported her, like he always did with her crazy ideas. But after the goats arrived, it was obvious that none of us had any idea what we were getting ourselves into.

Hundreds of Spanish/Boer crossbred meat goats scattered across the grounds of Rush Creek next to the headquarters of the barn and the corrals. Oh, and don't forget the Nubian milk goats we had acquired with the group. After we figured out that three hundred was way too many, we downsized to about thirty. Although the herd was smaller, they were still a pain in my ass.

Perfect. The ball in the bed of the pickup lined up with the trailer. The vehicle jolted a little when I put it in park, but we were still lined up OK. I swiftly connected the cables and cranked the trailer jack. I had picked the gooseneck because I knew I would be able to back it on my own. I wasn't about to let Mom help me with the bumper pull. Today was already stressful enough, and I didn't need to add to that.

In the home, Mom was the boss. She ran the house, cooked our meals, ironed our clothes, and held down a job that had insurance. I respected her in that position, but outside, in my realm of the world, I had zero patience with her skills. I understood how she felt when I refused to make my bed or didn't see the beauty of a well-kept home. Washed walls and shiny floors weren't of importance to me. But taking care of animals? That was my job.

Since I was only ten years old at the time, Mom insisted she drive on the county roads. She didn't want me to wreck the work truck and risk having an underaged driver. Though I had done it many times before, I agreed to the idea.

As we arrived, the neighbors directed us to the pasture.

And there they were.

This had become such a common occurrence that I was still unsure why we had the pesky little shits. All they did was run away and cause problems. They. Were. Everywhere. If you've ever seen a reckless toddler, imagine a group of them gathered together in a united front to completely tear you down, physically and mentally. They were Houdini escape artists, never ceasing to take the opportunity to flee. Their diet consisted of garbage, feed, and goathead stickers. And their personalities? Oof. The world was their playground, and unfortunately that meant our vehicles, our wood piles, and anything else that resembled a deconstructed jungle gym.

Mom pulled off the county road onto a two-track, careful not to drive on their grass. Dad had warned me several times about doing this, so I directed Mom where to drive. I prayed that no one would come outside to see what was about to go down. We were a God damn hot mess.

Mom looked so unnatural chasing them, flailing her hands about in the air. I wondered if the neighbors could see us in the pasture from our house. I imagined the television captions that would accompany our frenzy.

[Heavy breathing]

[Unintelligible yelling]

[Goat bleating]

We had no leverage, but I had a trick up my sleeve I knew would work. Goats are ruthless, but they're easily fooled. I laid down pieces of cake I had stolen from the cattle stores by the barn. I took the large feed pellets and made a trail leading up the trailer, dumping the rest in the front of their ride home. They were easily lured.

One goat, two goats, three goats…

Hop, hop, hop. They pranced inside the trailer to find their treats.

"Hurry, Mom!" I yelled at her to close the gate behind them.

Another day's work, zero dollars to show for it.

Every day, I traveled two miles from the house on my four-wheeler to take care of them. They weren't allowed near the house anymore because of the damage they inflicted on anything they came near. I watched my mamas birth many babies into the world. Some of my older nannies were having triplets and even quads. Most never had singles anymore—only twins. It's funny how life works out, because it seems I had been working with multiples long before I ever had my own. Every evening, I would feed the goats and lock them in their pen overnight. It was a relief when they were there when I showed up, because who knew where they went during the daytime hours. And when mamas started having babies, it was exhausting. They were always hiding their kids during the day and leaving them there. When I locked them up at night, there were often a few missing babies. And guess who had to find them if they didn't show up? You guessed it. This girl.

I would take the four-wheeler all over the radius of the goat pens, searching for the babies. If you've ever seen a baby goat, you will understand how tiny they are. They were about the size of rabbits. Dad would make me search until it got dark. Some days, the babies were never found, and I would hope and pray that their moms would go find them the next day. This game we played was so tiresome.

There were days my four-wheeler broke down. Sometimes it would break down two miles out, and sometimes it broke down farther away because I would find the goats somewhere they weren't supposed to be. I remember walking home in the rain, in the dark, sometimes even hiding behind sagebrush as I walked to avoid the crazy cattle that lurked in the horse trap. These goats caused me so many problems, and my parents continued to make me take care of them!

As we drove our herd of goats home to our land, I knew it wouldn't be the last time this happened. It was only a matter of time before they ran away again.

In a roundabout way, I had been chasing "kids" since long before I had my own children. Having a herd of goats and helping Dad run three thousand head of cattle is still nothing compared to the challenges of motherhood, but it's pretty damn close.

October 2022

The twins pulled at my pant leg as I entered grades. Don't get me wrong, I loved my new schedule and being home with my kids. But my days were *wild*. I turned cartoons on to keep them occupied while I was in a meeting, and before I knew it, I could see

Baby A behind me on the table hanging from the chandelier. I wish I was making this up, but he actually climbed onto our dining room table and decided to try his trapeze skills. Luckily, my coworkers found it hilarious rather than distracting.

The meeting ended, and I assessed the room for more damage. Baby B had shit on the floor. Again, you can't make this shit up. This wasn't the first time it had happened, either. I had feral nudists living in the house with me, and it was part of my job to keep them alive, all while teaching the public youth. I asked God if He could lay off of the challenges for a while. Like, could I just get one day of calm? Maybe instead of a baby hanging from the chandelier *and* shit on the floor, we could just choose one or the other?

It was strange, because my workload was a lot lighter working from home, but it takes a special mentality not to let the chaos in the house get to you. The messes are always there, right in front of you. The kids are always there—like *right there*. I can't describe how happy I was to make this move for my family, but I was also wondering if I would ever be able to write a book under these circumstances.

It was absolute chaos.

But maybe I worked best in chaos. Maybe I needed the pressure to help me start writing my book.

During my lunch break, I happened to stumble upon a video of another author preparing for something called NaNoWriMo. I had never heard of it.

Nap time rolled around, and I collapsed on my bed, checking my work emails and opening student assignments to grade. Once I was finished, I found myself on Google.

NaNoWriMo, a challenge to write a fifty thousand-word rough draft in the month of November. Hmm... It sounded chaotic. Why not?

I was tired of waiting, and I decided it was time. The whole reason I'd started applying for new jobs was to write a book. If I could herd goats all over eastern Colorado and live to tell the tale, there was no reason I couldn't do this.

I opened my social media and began to write a post.

"I am about to do something crazy, guys!"

The boys giggled in their cribs, reminding me I had just spent half of my nap time break researching NaNoWriMo. When I opened their bedroom door, they were smirking, almost like they knew that I was up to something. They were ready to wreck me, testing every ounce of my patience.

Here I go again, herding kids, I thought to myself.

CHAPTER TWENTY-FOUR

THE TWINS SHRIEKED IN PAIN. TYLENOL AND MOTRIN bottles lined our countertops, and syringes lay scattered around the house. This was their first ear infection, and of course they happened simultaneously. Twins never do anything alone, after all.

The nights were long, and we performed something I like to call the baby shuffle. One baby would get up, we would get him settled down, then the next would wake up, and we would start all over. It was an ongoing dance until the daylight saved us from the never-ending night.

The weather was getting cooler, and I could feel the season of sickness upon us. I hadn't realized how long we'd been inside after the boys were born. This was the first year they were out in the world of germs. They were born in the midst of a global pandemic, so the whole "going out and about" thing was still new to our family.

It was perfect timing too, because I had just decided to write a fifty thousand-word rough draft, right smack in the middle of the boys' illnesses. What was my life without a little madness, right?

The pain seemed to subside over a few days, and their antibiotics ran out. The experience gave me flashbacks to the newborn days, and I trembled with the trauma that lingered from the experience. How did I survive not sleeping for that long?

Their ear infections eclipsed my first week of NaNoWriMo. I was severely behind, and the competition had just started. I knew that if I didn't write this book now, I never would. I just wasn't sure how I would finish when I was only writing a thousand or so words a day. I had a lot of ground to catch up.

I wrote on my phone during cuddles, in bed before I went to sleep, and in small sprints when my husband was home from work. I was still lagging behind in the challenge.

The following week, we found ourselves back in the doctor's office. The boys' ear infections were back, and they were put on another ten days of antibiotics. Between the shrieking and the diarrhea, I couldn't hear myself think. I was barely able to function, and my rough draft languished in my Google Drive, waiting to be finished.

Finding the time to finish this challenge was a battle, but it was also a blessing. Until now in my writing journey, I had been in analysis paralysis. When you have no time to think, it's easier to get the words on paper. I was writing pure nonsense, but the word count continued to slowly rise.

Thanksgiving break was right around the corner. One week to really hit the keyboard hard. Would I be able to finish?

My goat pooped all over himself.

We were seriously two competition classes away from the meat goat class, and he had shit all down his leg. Apparently I wasn't the only one getting nervous diarrhea. This was it—the county fair. All the hard work I'd put in culminated in one goat show.

I'd participated in 4-H all my life. The amount of work that we all put into the animals we showed was impressive. We were just children, but we cared for animals, trained them, and put ourselves out there in a ring full of judges.

Dad rushed back to the goat pens and had no choice but to wipe my goat's ass for me. I was mortified. He knew how important that day was to me. I'd worked so hard with both of my goats, and no poop-stained Chevon was going to win me Grand Champion.

They called us into the show ring, and I put my game face on. I trusted Dad would do what he needed to do, because at this point I was in the showmanship class with my other goat.

Although I was only twelve years old at the time, I meant some serious business. My parents had taken me to clinics, and I'd worked countless hours in the pens taming my feral goats.

The judge walked around scanning the animals, and my eyes stuck to him like glue. Each time he passed, I switched sides, keeping the animal between me and the judge. This wasn't about me; it was about my showmanship.

I listened for instructions as the judge directed us to move our animals in various positions around the show ring. My goat strutted and let me touch his legs no problem. We'd practiced this for many hours by the barn. My goat trusted me and no longer feared my touch.

He lined me up second to a boy who was a senior in high school. I had just won Reserve Champion Showman, beating all of the other high schoolers. They handed us our ribbons and we were directed out of the show ring.

The uneasy feeling in my stomach started all over again as I prepared for my next event.

Did Dad get the poop off his legs?

Dad was waiting for me with a reassuring smile, my goat's legs pretty and white, not even a speck of dirt showing. I still had a chance at a Grand Champion ribbon, and I knew the meat goat class was my time to shine.

All the stars aligned and my goat looked magnificent. He stood flexed, his white coat glimmering in the morning sun. His shaved body accentuated the muscles we'd built together. The exercise regime included twenty-five climbs on the loading ramp, occasional runs in the round pen, and running sprints back to their feed. This combined with a high-calorie diet and love made an ideal goat to butcher.

The judge walked toward me once again, and I took a deep breath. The smell of wood shavings and animal poop filled my nose, and I relaxed my body. He measured the loin with his hand and studied my goat's muscular glutes. I braced my arm against the chain so my goat would flex even more. I knew he looked damn good; he'd eaten well the night before and didn't swell with bloat like some animals did.

As the judge started to direct the kids into their placing, I was the last to be called. I knew exactly why. This time, I was in the front of the line. I was the Grand Champion. I don't even remember smiling, but I do remember looking out past the judge into the stands and seeing Dad's thumbs up. I knew I earned that ribbon, and he knew it too.

The twins devoured Mom's chocolate chip pie at Thanksgiving dinner. Their smiles, full of brown chocolate, disgusted me and made me laugh at the same time. It was a nice feeling to see my kids happy again. The entire month had been a marathon of screaming, antibiotics, and pain meds. My mental toughness was the lowest it had been since our NICU days. I had taken the last week to catch up on the challenge of NaNoWriMo and celebrated my progress with my own plate of chocolate chip pie and an unreasonable amount of mashed potatoes. I wasn't a huge fan of the traditional Thanksgiving foods, but I was always down for a pile of potatoes covered in ham gravy.

The hard work and perseverance was paying off, and I was happy I hadn't given up two weeks ago. It was difficult to write in the middle of double ear infection rage, but it was worth it to finally get my story on the pages in front of me. The hardest part was starting, and I was almost done with my fifty thousand-word rough draft.

As we left Thanksgiving dinner, the boys fell asleep in the car. Their full bellies, along with the excitement of seeing family, had them pooped. I crossed my fingers that this would be the hardest part of our winter. I thought maybe since we'd had two ear infections, our time was up.

Wrong.

The following day, Mom and I went out to explore some Black Friday shopping, gearing up for the holiday season. The small market we entered was fairly busy, crafts and small businesses scattered throughout the venue. The happy boys I'd seen yesterday at Thanksgiving dinner were not so happy today. The hum of holiday cheer and chatter went from exciting and jolly to overwhelming. The twins' whines started to make my eyes twitch. I knew I couldn't get to the end of this challenge that easily.

I was one week away from my deadline for NaNoWriMo, and this situation felt all too familiar. After all that hard work, my goat shit all over himself right at the finish line. I was thousands of words away from completing a first draft, and this time I didn't have Dad there to save the day.

If the boys were sick, there was nothing I could do about it. At the same time, I knew this was just one small hurdle standing in the way of all the hard work I had accomplished in the month of November. I didn't let the goat shitting all over himself ruin the rest of the show. I followed through and I made sure to finish what I started.

It was going to be difficult, but my draft would not be a word short of fifty thousand on November 30.

CHAPTER TWENTY-FIVE

NOVEMBER 2022

THE FOLLOWING MONDAY, WE FOUND OURSELVES BACK IN the doctor's office for the third time in November. The waiting room was full of coughing kids that sounded just like mine. The sound of snot being sucked back into their noses made me realize we weren't the only ones going through this hell.

Over the weekend, Baby A had seemed to fight the virus on his own, but Baby B screamed in agony, and I knew something was off. When he threw his head back and put his ear to the ground, searching for relief, I made the decision to get my ass to the doctor. I knew what that meant.

We waited forever, the boys both wanting to be held. Their wagon filled with snacks, tablets, toys, and a place for them to lie down wasn't appealing to them. My lap was their only comfort, and I found myself awkwardly trying to hold both toddlers.

The nurse and the doctor arrived, apologizing for the wait. They poked and prodded Baby B, swabbing his saliva and taking his temperature. His face turned red in anger, and his cough was weak when he couldn't calm himself down.

"He tested positive for RSV, and he has another ear infection." She looked at me with remorse as she delivered the news. I was ready for the ear infection diagnosis, but I wasn't really thrilled about the RSV. It's a respiratory virus we'd been warned about since we left the NICU. Kiddos often end up in the hospital with it, and I cringed at the thought of being there again.

I drove to the pharmacy after our appointment to get what we needed and prayed that he would get over the virus on his own. I was alone, of course. That's usually how my luck works out. I took the afternoon to gather myself and focus on what I could control.

Tylenol, Motrin, water, and cuddles were my only weapons in the fight to help him feel better. As the day moved along, Baby B's fever increased from 101 to 103 degrees. I stayed calm, pushing the fever reducers, but after three rounds, his temperature still wasn't going down. His breathing became raspy and he lay on my lap continuing to get worse.

I had downplayed my own symptoms before, and that had landed all three of us in a Flight For Life helicopter. I wasn't taking that chance ever again. I called my husband and told him to meet me at the hospital across from the fire station where he worked. I called my mother-in-law to stay with Baby A as I loaded us into the car. Baby B's breathing was becoming more labored, and his body was on fire.

I turned off the radio in the car so I could listen closely to his breathing. The sound wasn't rhythmic; it wasn't steady. I focused on listening and seeing the road at the same time. For some reason, I felt like I couldn't do both at once. I was too worried.

As I pulled into the hospital parking lot, I drove to the front entrance, but before I could park I got a phone call from Josh.

"Keep driving. Don't ask questions, just drive."

"What the hell is going on, Josh?!"

"Kelcie, just come around the back and keep driving!"

The fact that he gave no explanation sent me into panic and rage. *What the actual fuck?* Here I was, afraid my kid couldn't breathe, and someone was dropping another bomb on me with little context. Lord have mercy.

I pulled around the back, where Josh had used his badge to get us the VIP treatment in the ER. As he unloaded Baby B from the car, I demanded an explanation for the creepy phone call.

"There was a guy with a gun at the front entrance. You literally drove right past him. They had the hospital on lockdown to be sure he wouldn't get in here," Josh angry-whispered at me as we entered the hospital.

"Oh hell, of all nights," I angry-whispered back, not letting the nurse see that we were bickering. I tried not to think about how I could have just gotten shot while trying to take care of my kid, but when you're a mom, not even dying scares you. You just focus on getting your kid to safety.

The inside of the ER was full. A nurse directed us to a room to get vitals, and the minute we got there, Baby B's breathing calmed and his fever started to go down. Of course. The nurse scribbled some notes and gave him another dose of fever reducers.

Baby B's eyes drooped, the bags weighing his expression down. He sat on the hospital bed, not trying to escape like usual. It was so loud, and there weren't any chairs to sit in. We were packed into a triage room, the ER still overflowing with sickness. They were getting us in and out as fast as they could, but there still weren't enough regular patient rooms for us to wait.

The beepers, the machines, and the masked personnel brought back memories of the NICU. The times that were beautiful for most new parents in a hospital had scarred me. A pit formed in my stomach as I realized that it wasn't that long ago that we were prisoners in a hospital. The very place that saves lives had also caused me so much heartache.

The doctor walked in, scanning a clipboard.

"The cold air probably helped his lungs and brought his fever down," she explained. He still wasn't in great shape; definitely not the wild secondborn hellion I was used to. He lay there exhausted, waiting for her to leave him alone so he could go back to sleep.

"You did the right thing. These little ones can turn fast, and this year has been the worst year for respiratory illnesses," the doctor reassured me. Truthfully, I didn't care that the ER trip might not have been necessary. I was GLAD he was better, and I would make the same decision if it happened again. When it came to my kids, I would never take risks again. The traumatic birth experience may have been hard on me, but it taught me never to second guess your intuition. If something feels off, it probably is.

His breathing wasn't as labored as when I left the house, but it still wasn't great. She ordered a CAT scan of his lungs to make sure he didn't have pneumonia as well. Because there were no rooms left, we were directed to the waiting room. He never opened his eyes as we got him situated to move. He grasped at the collar of his dad's shirt, his mouth open to breathe and his cheeks rosy from his fever.

I followed behind him, diaper bag, water bottle, tablet, and snacks in tow. The open waiting room made me cringe. It was a sight into our city that was hard to see. People who seemed to be homeless lay on the floor, and there were other patients who were clearly on some type of drugs. They paced back and forth, looking out the glass window. I remembered the man with a gun and backed us into a corner opposite the window so I could see outside.

Kids and babies sat in their mothers' arms, pitiful and help-less. I looked into other mothers' eyes and saw the worry and the exhaustion. It was almost midnight in the middle of one of the roughest parts of town, and I knew we weren't getting into that CAT scan any time soon.

I had three days left of NaNoWriMo, and in the midst of

more chaos, I pulled out my phone and started writing. I was determined to finish my book.

The bath water ran as my sister Kylie held a half dead baby goat in her arms. It had been born a few days ago, when the spring snow came with bad intentions. No matter the animal, the weather always sent us into calving, or in this case, kidding spurts. Baby goats were hitting the ground, and my old mamas were all having twins and triplets. We had one set of quads that year as well. Their tiny bodies were tough, but this time, the cold had frozen down one of our babies near death.

Dad usually carried the patients inside, calling us to come and do our magic. That day, our patient was a tiny baby goat. Many cold animals were resuscitated back to life in our homes, and this one was getting the Smith girl treatment. We knew the drill.

"Mom! Where's the blow-dryer?!" I yelled as Kylie ran the warm water over the baby goat popsicle. She got inside the bathtub with the dirty little thing, petting it and kissing it. The kid resembled a small dog, her coat white and her head reddish brown in color. She was breathing, but we weren't sure if we could save this one. She had been out in the cold for a while now.

"Kylie, dry her off with this towel while I get the blow-dryer going," I directed my sister. My sister was around four and I was around ten years of age. Over the few years we'd had goats, we had figured out a system. Even though we usually fought all day long, when it came to the animals, we put all of our fighting aside. I thought she was going to squeeze the poor animal to death, but I remembered that was part of our method for bringing them back to life—unconditional love. The blow-dryer roared in our bathroom as we got her nice and warm. She seemed to be thawing out now.

I heard the screen door slam and I jumped up to see if Dad had brought us another. I met him at the door, his hands full of supplies.

"Two scoops," he said as he handed me the powdered goat formula. I set it down by the washer and dryer and grabbed the beer bottle and nipple from his hands.

"Got it," I replied. He had more ice to break for the cattle, but we had everything we needed to help our patient as best we could. When he shut the door behind him, I started running some warm water to mix the formula with. Kylie sat in the bathroom cuddling the baby goat in blankets.

I held my breath as I funneled the stinky formula into the empty beer bottle. I took the full bottle and covered it with my thumb to shake. The nipple was new, and I had to finesse it over the top of the bottle. I was praying the poor goat would eat.

My sister wouldn't leave her side. She sat beside the box we'd put her in and watched her sleep. We offered her a bottle every few hours, and eventually she was eating the full serving. The tiny goat defrosted and came back to life.

I watched as Kylie took the lead in taking care of the baby. She was attached to the little creature, acting like it was one of her baby dolls. Just like a baby, she cared for it. When she replaced the newspaper in her box, she would call it "changing her diaper." My sister was so dedicated that she took the baby with her to my Grammy's house, where we kept her in the laundry room. She claimed it as her own.

The little popsicle thawed and became our pet. Cutie was her name. When she got bigger, she wasn't allowed inside anymore, but she lived in the yard with our dog. She played and pranced and cuddled with our border collie any chance she got! So much so that, after a while, I think Cutie thought she was also a dog.

When visitors came over, she went up to them asking for cuddles and kisses. It was a bizarre thing to see an animal that usually annoyed me become our family pet. We saved her—we brought that little goat back to life. Nurturing was in our hearts.

When they warn you about motherhood being hard, they warn you about all of the physical challenges. They say bottles, changing diapers, and behaviors will be the death of you. What really takes a toll on you is the mental aspect—the worry you feel. The love that's so strong it hurts. That's what they don't warn you about.

I took care of babies. I brought animals back to life. But I had never loved something so much that it felt like a projection of my heart outside of my body. If something happened to them, it physically and mentally hurt me. Their cries break your heart, because the mere thought of them in any discomfort hurts you. You're their mom!

I always thought that I would be a good mom because of what I learned taking care of animals, but it wasn't just the blood, sweat, and tears that made me a good mother. It was the emotional heartache that I felt when we lost animals. It was the realization that death is real, and that there's nothing you can do to change nature's mind. There's nothing you can do to control God's will.

My childhood was full of learning the responsibilities of taking care of life and respecting it. I wasn't a stranger to the hard work it took to keep another living being alive. Dad made sure of that.

In motherhood, we are oftentimes looking for a means to an end. *They'll eventually be easier to take care of. They'll eventually be able to tell us what's wrong. When we get done with diapers, it'll get easier. When they can dress themselves, I'm sure things will go faster when we try to get out of the house.*

The truth is, there is no end. When you become a parent, you sign up for a lifetime. You continue to show up. Every. Single. Day. I decided a long time ago that I wasn't going to wait for things to "get easier." If I did that, I would never do the things I wanted to do. Instead, I buckled down.

When we got the news that Baby B was clear of pneumonia, we went home. I had two days left to complete NaNoWriMo. I knew that it would be easier to push through the next two days than it would be to know that I didn't finish.

The last stretch of November tested my tenacity, but it also led to my growth in becoming an author.

CHAPTER TWENTY-SIX

The roping steers made their way through the chutes, pushing their heads away as we put on their protective headgear. One at a time, we put the steers through the chute, letting them out to see who would win—them or the cowboys?

The roping arena Dad created at Rush Creek headquarters was a playground for his friends and our neighbors. They gathered leisurely, practicing their skills on trained small Corriente steers. They still had horns, and they were a perfect way to blow off some steam.

Cowboys held their coils and reins in one hand, their loops in the other. I watched as they backed their horses into the rubber-lined corners of the roping box. The header of the group always lined up on the left-hand side of the chute. He would be the first roper to throw his loop, catching the steer around the horns. I watched him closely, tiptoeing to get my eyes above the steer's back, waiting for the header's signal.

He nodded.

I swiftly pulled the rope, opening the gate for the steer to jolt forward. Both horses flew past me, their hooves grabbing the dirt below them. The rest was a coin flip. If the header missed the horns, it was over, but if he landed a catch, the pressure was on the heeler. He would aim for the feet to stretch the steer, signifying a qualifying run in the rodeo world.

Team ropers in pro rodeo do this as a sport to win big jackpots. On the ranch, it's how we take care of animals in the open pasture. Imagine you're sick and the doctor comes to you to give you medicine rather than having you travel to the emergency room to be prodded and exposed to others. We were the cattle's on-call doctors, and although we did this for sport, it was also practice for day-to-day work. If you miss your loop in an open field, you have to keep trying.

The header pulled the steer forward, making him run and hop in a rhythm. The heeler would swing with the same rhythm, waiting for the hop he could catch him in. A lot of times they failed, but when the two came together to make a catch, it was pretty slick. I watched out of curiosity, but eventually Dad bought me my own rope.

The metal roping dummy followed, and I practiced with Dad by the shop in our downtime. I rolled my tiny wrist round and round, focusing on the horns inside my loop on each pass. With a swing and release, the rope caught the head. I took my right hand and pulled the rope as fast as I could, and the loop shrunk and tightened around the metal horns. My smile radiated as I looked at Dad. I ran away like it was an actual steer, dragging it for Dad to get the heels. When he caught it, we cheered together.

Riding, swinging a rope—these things came naturally to me, and I enjoyed the time I had with Dad. It seemed like I was meant to be a cowpoke on Rush Creek, and the challenge of it all was exciting. The more I practiced, the better I got. Dad guided me, making sure my coils were held correctly and my loop the correct size. He made sure the distance between my long fingers and the honda was appropriate, and watched my release as I let my loop fly through the air.

There are so many moving parts while roping. You're

watching the target and swinging simultaneously. The biggest challenge is letting it become natural, and not allowing your brain to take over and overthink. Muscle memory is key.

The quality time roping the dummy with Dad was easy practice. I was getting pretty damn good. I got so good that Dad entered me in a competition for kids at his team roping event in Denver.

Mom made sure I looked spiffy, and I was up against a bunch of boys. The competition was held on a tile floor with a roping dummy similar to mine. All of us started on tile number one, closest to the roping dummy. If you caught, you moved on to the next tile, and if you missed, you were out. I continued to get farther and farther away from the dummy until it was just me and another little boy my age.

I swung my rope—step and release. I only caught one horn. The little boy went after me and caught both. I went up and gave him a high five. I was pissed that I lost to a boy, but the fancy new rope bag they brought out for my second-place finish brightened my mood.

Later in my life, I watched as my sister rode in a horseman show, and Dad pointed out a young man on horseback.

"Remember the boy who beat you in that roping competition? That's him." He pointed across the arena. Of course I remembered! I was happy to see he was still swinging his rope, but I was so confused about myself. During my childhood I'd tried so many things, and I was good at many, but I was never someone who had just ONE thing they liked doing. I did them all.

November 2022

I woke up late. I was surprised that the twins weren't up yet. I didn't hear any chatter from their room, and I realized everyone must have slept through the night. *Finally.* I looked over at an empty bed, remembering that Josh was back on shift. I didn't even hear him leave for work—not his morning pee or his feet shuffling around, and I sure as hell didn't hear him stoke the stove for our percolator coffee. When I got up, I could smell it in the air. Phew. I needed some, stat.

The last day of November—the last day of NaNoWriMo—was here. The boys had healed tremendously in the past twenty-four hours since Baby B came home from the ER. It seemed like I had been running on empty all month. Three ear infections and a trip to the hospital was not how I'd envisioned things going. Now that we seemed to be out of the woods, I realized how much I had been holding in to survive the month.

With the chronic ear infections, we were referred to a specialist to see if we could get the boys surgery. That was coming up at the end of December. We also had an early interventionist come to our house to evaluate the boys' speech. They weren't talking yet, and we assumed it had a lot to do with their hearing, but we needed to get speech therapy going as soon as possible to help them after surgery. The list of appointments and worries started stacking up.

I had exactly one thousand words left to write, and I avoided them all day long. I found anything and everything I could to keep from finishing NaNoWriMo. The boys lounged around the house, not at full battery level yet, but getting there. Their cartoons rolled by on the TV and I found myself cleaning, even folding laundry. I was procrastinating, and I couldn't figure out why. I guess I was brain dead after the month I'd just had.

For some reason, November seemed to be a month of change

for me. It had been every year since 2020. My twins were born early, then the next November I decided I wanted something different in my career, and now here I was in the thick of writing a book while trying to keep my kids healthy. Maybe I should just lock myself inside next November?

While the boys were asleep, I decided I needed some fresh air. I needed to clear my head and find the motivation to write my last thousand words. I laid out the boys' hoodies and shoes. Outside, the air compressor roared, the tires on their stroller lifting off the ground. Walking was such a regular thing for us, and we hadn't been able to enjoy it since they'd started getting sick.

When I turned off the air compressor, I could hear them inside jabbering to each other in their own twin language. I knew they needed this walk too. I left the door into the garage open on purpose, putting their shoes on inside their room. Once they saw their exit, they ran, climbing inside their stroller. The garage door lifted, and the rays of sun blinded us. We were like Dracula coming out of his coffin. The air was as crisp as the fallen leaves, and the stress seemed to melt away.

Gravel crunched under the tires. We left our driveway to enjoy the prettiest parts of where we lived. Pumpkins rotted in the fields, the leaves had fallen from the trees, and we would soon be bracing ourselves for the cold of winter.

My phone stayed inside the stroller's storage compartment, only there in case of emergency. No music played, no one spoke, and we enjoyed the voices of nature.

As I continued to walk, I kept hearing a phrase repeat in my mind. I was supposed to be clearing my thoughts, but I kept hearing it. It was like a song you can't get out of your head.

"Little cowpoke, little cowpoke, spurs and black hat, how did you learn to swing a rope just like that?"

For the entire mile, I continued to hum the little tune in my head. The rhythm of our walking created a cadence for me to follow. I remember reading a book by Elizabeth Gilbert called *Big Magic*. She described the universe speaking to you and bringing you big magic. If you pushed it away, it would find someone else. It would find someone who was ready to bring that magic to life.

I turned around at the end of our side road and began to power walk.

I continued to hum the phrase over and over so I wouldn't forget it.

Then a second verse came to me. When you're a writer, these thoughts always seem to come to you when you're away from your materials. I watched the boys' heads bobble as I hit a few bumps. They didn't seem to mind.

I ran inside as soon as we got home from our walk, and within minutes I had a children's book sitting next to my rough draft for NaNoWriMo.

What the hell was I getting myself into this time?

The work I was doing to keep my boys healthy and on track developmentally was weighing on me, but I allowed myself that small little victory. I couldn't believe what I was doing. It felt similar to the feeling of swinging a rope for the first time. It felt natural. But it was a completely different genre from what I was writing now. I thought back to the ranch. Sometimes it was frustrating that my brain never seemed to be satisfied. I wondered why I couldn't be like the kid who'd beat me at the roping competition, always working toward mastering one thing. Again, I found myself comparing myself to others, looking for happiness in being like everyone else.

I pushed the negativity away. This children's book idea was meant to be mine. Right after I wrote it, I finished my fifty thousand words. Big Magic had found me, and I chose to embrace it. My memoir was my therapy project—my way of hashing out who I wanted to be. This children's book was the spark of fun I needed to finish my rough draft.

On November 30, I sat at my table with a rough draft of a

memoir and a notebook with a children's book scribbled in it. Yet again, I had a new challenge ahead of me.

CHAPTER TWENTY-SEVEN

WE STEPPED INTO ANOTHER DOCTOR'S OFFICE, GRABBING masks as we walked through the doors. The lengthy paperwork we had to fill out while wrangling two toddlers in the waiting room was enough to piss anyone off. I reached to the depths of my patience, scrolling through the checklists on the iPad they'd given me while my kids climbed up and down all the chairs.

The Christmas festivities had passed in a flash, and we were just a few days away from the New Year. I decided to take the month of December off from writing. November almost killed me, and I wanted writing to be a positive in my life, not something that burned me out.

I looked at the walls of the doctor's office. I was really over the white paint. First of all, it was ugly, and second of all, it was triggering, reminding me of every other white-walled doctor's office I had been in. Pick a different color!

I couldn't explain how I was feeling. I wanted them to find something wrong with the boys' ears so we knew why they weren't talking. But I also didn't want anything to be wrong with their ears, because what if they had to wear hearing aids? Because if their ears were fine, then why wouldn't they speak?

The mental shit show of motherhood continued to beat me down. Everyone said it would get easier, but I felt like we were right back where we started. We were in a hospital, without answers, praying that the boys would be OK. There are worse things that could have been wrong with our kids, but it didn't make it any less difficult. There were very brief moments we got to enjoy them instead of constantly worrying about them.

Corralling toddler twins into all of the different rooms had me sweating. The audiologist took one second in each ear to notice that there weren't any waves coming back from the tympanogram test that checked to see if their eardrums were working correctly. She explained that the minute the sound hit the eardrums, it should bounce back to her little machine. There was nothing bouncing back.

It took five minutes for the doctor to see that they both had ears full of fluid and swollen tonsils. They needed their tonsils removed and their adenoids removed, as well as tubes put in their ears to drain the fluid. I also advocated for a sedated hearing test, which used sound waves and brain activity to see if the eardrum was working properly. I wanted to be certain there was no hearing loss. I'd learned in the NICU that just because you're working with professionals doesn't mean they'll always do what's best. They're humans too, and they don't know your child like you do. I wanted definite answers that their ears weren't damaged, and relying on nonverbal toddlers in a hearing test room was not accurate in my mind. Their ears had been infected for so long that it could have caused damage.

Josh and I sat in the room with the doctor holding our wriggling children, our faces cold. The doctor looked back at us, and even with his mask on, I still could see the look on his face.

"It's going to be hell for two weeks," the doctor told us dryly. I appreciated his honesty, but it wasn't what I wanted to hear. The past few months had already been hell, and I wasn't sure if I could take it anymore.

It would take two weeks of recovery for them to start feeling normal. Their tonsils wouldn't fully heal for another three months.

When the doctor left the room, I looked at my poor husband.

"Here we go again, huh?" I nudged Josh.

"No worse than anything we've been through so far..." he replied under his breath.

"Come on, Pokey!" Dad shouted at me from across the pasture.

"I'm hurrying!" I shouted back from my seat on my old gelding named 202. The truth is, I was doing something far from "hurrying." Cowpokes like me never take their seasoned ponies out of 4-low, the lowest, slowest gear. The diaper bag and our water bottles hung secured to my saddle horn, seeming to slow me down even more. The water sloshed around, and the diaper bag swung back and forth beside my left leg as I broke into a trot. My small figure bobbed up and down as I closed the gap between us.

Dad was on Whitey that day, and a baby sling was strapped to his back. As he turned toward me, I could see my little sister, her big ears sticking out from underneath her denim bucket hat. She smiled so big as I rode up to them with our supplies.

Mom had gone back to work as a prison guard. Her hours seemed to change often, and shift work made Dad our sole care-taker during the daytime hours. I was homeschooled, so I had no choice but to help Dad with my firecracker sister.

After our snack break, I put my game face on. You have to understand, I was the slowest cowpoke on this planet. The grass grew faster than I moved. You know what, though? It worked for us. Dad sifted through the pasture with my sister in a slow gallop, gathering cattle and aiming them in the general direction of where we were going. And I—well, I basically used my slow, calming presence to herd the cattle in the same direction. I did my best! My methods didn't get things done very quickly, but they were effective.

We moved a couple hundred head that day all by ourselves. I was so focused on doing my job as the snack holder/cowpoke that I never realized how important that moment in time was. I had a father who was willing to take his nine- and three-year-old girls on horseback across the pastures we refer to as God's Country. I had a mother who trusted and loved Dad enough to leave him with her two babies. She went on to climb her way to the rank of sergeant at the prison.

Experiences like this gave me high expectations for the partner I would choose to spend the rest of my life with. These experiences also held me accountable for my own actions as I entered a relationship with my husband.

When I met Josh, I knew that he would take me for who I was. I was raised without gender roles, and meeting someone who respected that was special to me. We were equals in our relationship, and it made our teamwork intense. I remember someone once telling me that a good relationship isn't fifty-fifty —a good relationship is each person giving 100 percent. I knew that no matter the circumstances, Josh would give his all, just as I would.

When you're raising children, it's important to have someone who's willing to go through the hard stuff with you. Sometimes it gets ugly, and sometimes it means one of you is making sacrifices so their partner can have a break. Josh had been there for me since day one. He paid all of our bills when I was battling through my college degree. He picked up the slack when I was puking my guts up during pregnancy. He even hired help to come over when the boys were young so I could get some sleep while he was on shift at the fire department. There really isn't anything he wouldn't do for me.

I had supported his mental health for the past year by taking the work-from-home position. But this surgery weighed heavily on my mind, and dark thoughts from the NICU were beginning to resurface. The thought of the boys being put under, being in pain, and not sleeping again felt debilitating. My mind and my body couldn't take it anymore. I knew I would need Josh more than ever in the month of January, when my boys would return to the hospital for surgery.

CHAPTER TWENTY-EIGHT

It was surgery day. As we rumbled onto the interstate, I was reminded of the same path we'd taken just two years ago. It was the same frosty weather and the same nauseous feeling. This time, my kids were in the car with me, and I could hardly imagine letting the medical staff take them back to surgery. I tried to hide my anxiety from Josh, but the tension in the air was palpable.

The boys had no clue what was about to happen, and it broke my heart to see their groggy smiles as we unloaded them from the pickup. The boys' surgeries were scheduled back-to-back. They would last ninety minutes each—sedated hearing tests, adenoid removal, tonsil removal, and tube insertion in their ears. They sat on the bed together in their little hospital gowns, only their diapers on underneath. The waiting seemed like an eternity.

We were at a different hospital, but the same white walls closed in. I always felt like they blinded and deafened me all at once. Maybe they kept the walls this color so you didn't have the mental space to think about what was going on. We had two rooms allotted to us, but we all crammed in one to be together. I longed for the NICU, where I was familiar with the staff and the protocol. We were just here for the day, and I felt like a stranger. I *was* a stranger to most of the staff.

Everything happened fast once we got there, but the minute they took Baby B, time slowed down. He was the first to go under. They distracted him with an iPad as they wheeled him away. I thought back to when they were born and I watched one being rolled away from me. I know parents with multiple children feel this way, but the twin mom thing really can hurt sometimes. It feels like your whole soul is being pulled in two directions when they're separated.

We waited with Baby A, ready to hear good news. I could hear his brother screaming in the room next to us. Well, he was alive. Screaming was always a good sign of breathing! We weren't allowed to go in until the medical staff cleared it, and I felt like yelling at the nurse I could hear trying to comfort him. Baby B was, and still is, my bull of a boy. He is sweet but stubborn, and he would do anything to get his point across. He wanted no one but his mom in that moment, and I stared at the staff outside our waiting room, convincing them with my eyes to let me in there.

It was perfect timing, because they took Baby A back as they let us into the room with his recovering brother. Baby B was angry. He thrashed, he hit, and he screamed so hard, we had to keep him on oxygen. As soon as I got him to calm down with a cartoon on his tablet, we saw Baby A being wheeled out of surgery.

Most parents don't see this part. Most parents only have one baby at a time and are confined to the waiting area. But once again, we weren't most parents.

His tiny body only took up a third of the hospital bed, but the oxygen mask took over his whole face. I could see his chest slowly moving. Up and down. Up and down. The wild man who often hung from my chandelier was now so still. My teeth squeaked, rubbing against each other. I didn't realize I was clenching so hard. I rubbed Baby B's back, waiting impatiently to get into the next room with his brother when he woke up.

That's when the alarm went off. My heart sank to my stomach. I felt a buzzing, like the thumping muscle was bouncing around, trying to find its way back to where it belonged. Just like in the NICU, I watched as the entire staff on the floor ran to my son's room. The crash cart was rolled in—the one they use when they're about to save someone's life. I knew what happened next.

I was pinned to the bed where my other son recovered, attached to cords and oxygen. Josh rapidly walked to the door. His Dad mode, along with his EMT mode, made for a tense body I was afraid to be near. I clung to his knowledge, and even though I knew we both knew what was happening, I asked the question, hopeful to hear different news.

"Is it his room? Is he OK?!" My voice trembled and tears ran down my face. I wasn't hearing; I struggled to breathe. Nerves tingled throughout my body, all of them sending out spurts of electricity with nowhere to go. The unused energy ended up in my throat, and I waited for them to tell me my Baby A was gone.

Josh wasn't answering me. He stared outside the room, waiting for someone to speak.

"Oh my God, is someone going to talk to us?! I can't hear anything!" My quavering voice was steeped in panic, and I tried to hold it back, noticing that Josh was using all of his strength not to smash through the glass door.

The next few minutes felt like an hour. I'm sure I held my breath the entire time. The room was dark this time, the lights dimmed for recovery. Drool ran down my arm. One twin slept while the other was surrounded by doctors. There was only one wall separating me from the truth. They only bring the AED in when they have to shock someone back to life. I'd seen them roll it in right in front of me. The loud staff went quiet, and I worried about what we would be told next.

"I am so sorry you had to see all of that!" A nurse walked into our room. She walked in too fucking calmly, not getting to the point.

"Is he OK?!" I demanded.

"Yes, he's fine. He just scared us a little, but everything is OK!" The nurse walked out, and the anesthesiologist walked in immediately after.

"His vocal cords started to spasm when he was waking up, so he stopped breathing for a little while. It happens! It's pretty common, but he's stable now," he explained.

"Well, we're a little freaked out since this isn't exactly the first time he's stopped breathing." I was relieved, but I also wondered why they wanted me to age prematurely. I could feel at least ten gray hairs and a clogged artery that had appeared in the past ten minutes.

Once we got both boys calm(er), we were in it for the long haul once again. The overnight stay in the hospital was horrible. The boys writhed in pain from their tonsils being removed, and my heart was still trying to find its way back from my stomach. There was no sleep, and there was a lot of worry. I found myself back in the survival mode I was in when they were newborns. I was just trying to make it out of there in one piece.

Mom sat in the recliner part of the couch, her computer plugged into the power outlet. Her perch was scattered with multiple drinks, papers, and books. It was Sunday, and all of her assignments were due at midnight. She was pursuing her credits to be a licensed teacher, working toward the end goal of her education administration degree.

Mom birthed three children and held a handful of different careers. She worked at Sam's Club, taught at the community college, took a position as a nursing home social worker, and just before my brother was born, she was a sergeant at the prison.

When I was five, she had my sister, and when I was eleven, she had my brother. In the space between each baby, she would start a new job as soon as we were old enough to go with Dad or go to school.

As my brother got older, a special education teaching position opened up at the school my sister and I attended. She jumped headfirst into an emergency license. I was old enough at that point to realize that meant the entire family was jumping in too.

Sunday was a figure-it-out-on-your-own day. Dad rested and watched TV, occasionally picking a movie to watch with us. Mom pounded away at the keyboard as we all took care of the house. She rarely spoke to us on Sunday unless she was yelling at us to ask our father.

Dad and I would make lunch and dinner and do our best to keep the house clean.

"Leave your mom alone, she's doing her school!" Dad yelled at the little ones while we browned the hamburger and cut vegetables for taco salad. The little ones were still needy, especially my brother, the baby. When my sister wasn't trying to bother my mom, she would bother me.

There were times I questioned if she ever got up to pee. That woman had to go hard, and it really confused me that she left it all until the very end to finish. She would literally turn in assignments at 11:58 when they were due at 11:59 p.m. Why did she do that to herself?

After having children, I realized why Mom always left all of her homework for Sunday. She was a MOM! She didn't have time during the week while being a full-time teacher and keeping up with all of our activities. Watching her climb the ranks at any job she took was something I will always be proud of. There was nothing that could stop her, and when she walked the halls as my superintendent, I knew that I could do anything and that nothing would ever get in my way.

On the days Mom had to set up camp on the couch to meet

her deadlines, I never once was mad at her. I never thought she was a bad mom. In fact, that was a time in my life when I was so proud of her. She was following her dreams, and Dad was supporting her. The kids were supporting her. That's what family is for.

———

When we got back from the hospital, I questioned my writing journey. When the alarms went off for Baby A, I thought I had lost him. Those five excruciating minutes completely crushed the momentum I had built up until this point in my motherhood and writing journey.

My anxiety was so high that I had to check multiple times a night that they were both breathing. All the work I had done to get out of my postpartum fog seemed to be for nothing. The guilt crept back in, and my worry would not subside. It didn't help that the boys weren't sleeping. We were up all night with them giving them pain meds. We were two years into parenthood, but it felt like we were right back at square one.

Two weeks passed, and their tonsils were starting to heal. We were slowly getting our sleep back. I had a rough draft that I needed to get to my professional editor. I thought about quitting again. I could just continue writing on my blog, maybe publish my children's book. But continuing to work on a full manuscript while being a parent just seemed like too much. I felt like I needed to spend more time with the boys, especially after what had just happened. But I thought back to how proud I was of Mom when she went after her dreams.

Their surgery mentally broke me, filling me with self-doubt. I was finding every excuse not to work on my book again. I had one month to figure out if I was going to continue this journey, or if I was going to throw in the towel.

CHAPTER TWENTY-NINE

I COULD HEAR MYSELF BREATHING. IT WASN'T BECAUSE I WAS stressed or vigorously exercising. It was just the ranch! It was so quiet that day. An occasional bird would chirp, but the air was so still—mute.

I waited inside the shop, a small building designated for mechanic jobs or leisure activities such as reloading bullets. It was a landing ground closest to the fuel tanks, the corrals, and the barn. Something in the air was uneasy; I could feel it. Dad hadn't sung any of his cheery songs, nor had he told me what we were going to do that day.

I scraped the dirty concrete floor with my boots, breaking the silence of the calm, stagnant air. I could hear the gate by the barn squeaking to open and close. The sound of Dad's footsteps walking down the alleyway seemed so clear, so loud. The usual chitchat of the morning was absent.

A small piece of wood had broken off the shop's sliding door. It was the perfect place for me to peek through as I anxiously anticipated the interaction that was about to take place. The hired hand was approaching the corrals. There were no greetings to be had, and I cringed. If Dad didn't tell you "Mornin'!" you must have really messed up.

The hired hand met Dad at the small entrance gate to the alley.

The ass-chewing commenced.

"Shut the f*%$#^* gate! We got cattle all over the GOT. DAMN. COUNTRY!"

Insert more profanity here

Dad took the small gate and repeatedly slammed it in front of the hired hand.

"IS IT THAT HARD TO CLOSE A GATE?!"

The hired hand didn't say a word. He didn't even try to justify what had happened, because he knew he had screwed up. My dad's anger radiated into the air. Even from a hundred yards away, I could see his red-stained sclera and the bulging blood vessel in the middle of his forehead. Words escaped his tightly clenched jaw. His white teeth, which usually signified joy and laughter, gleamed bright with rage.

The conversation cooled down, but Dad's teeth never unclenched. I still don't know what the hired hand had to do to make things right. All I know is we got in the pickup, Dad turned the radio on, and we drove off to complete a few daily chores.

That day, hours of work, miles of pasture, and the sweat of horses and men had all been wasted because one person forgot to shut a gate.

Now, when you read this story, you may think, "Well, that cowpoke won't ever forget to shut a gate again." But when I look back, that moment means something more to me.

I learned that throughout life, we pass through a lot of gates. Leaving them open is a bad habit that some of us, including me and the hired hand, tend to fall into. We may pass through a season of life, a relationship, or a hard time. These different places we've traveled through are an important part of our journey, but when they no longer serve us, we have to close the gate behind us. Could we need to go back there for something one day? Possibly. Are there memories and lessons we may have to revisit? Absolutely. But you want to do that on *your* terms. You don't want cattle—I mean the past—just running all over the GOT. DAMN. COUNTRY.

As we grow in life, we can't continue to leave gates open. If we do, all of our progress will escape us. Sometimes we want to go back to our old habits, maybe our old relationships, the person we were years ago. But why?

Every day, most of us are trying to better ourselves. We hurdle over these milestones in our life, and we forget to bring our progress with us! My dad may have lost his temper, and you may think he's a major asshole now, but you know what?

I'll never forget to close any gates.

February 2023

I accidentally left a gate open. Self-doubt made its way back in.

The bones of my house were still standing, but the inside was demolished. My kitchen island was our landing ground for pain meds, ear drops, syringes, and doctor's instructions. We had a tally of each twin's medicine dosages, times scribbled all over to try to keep the schedule straight. We didn't want to give them the wrong amount or the wrong medicine in our exhausted states.

I noticed there were small plastic containers under the couch. Since their tonsillectomy, their diet had consisted of individual cups of ice cream and small amounts of mac 'n' cheese. Nothing else. The melted sugar was sticky against our hardwood floor when I picked them up. I was trying to make a dent in the mess, but it seemed like every time I started cleaning one thing, I found something else.

The overwhelm set in. I felt like I would never recover from their surgery. They were healing, but our house was in shambles. I was in shambles. The mental load of motherhood started to weigh me down again. I thought I would soon be crushed if I didn't lighten the expectations for myself.

February was a big month for me, and I had to decide if I would continue with my revisions or save them for when I was "ready." I had also hired an illustrator for my children's book, but I wanted to quit that too. I constantly felt like I had taken on too much because of all of the expectations I placed on myself as a mother.

In the middle of the overwhelm, I sat on the couch, exhausted at the thought of getting my life together. There was no way I could continue writing. How? I know that a messy house doesn't seem like much, but for me, it made it feel like I couldn't move forward. I was still working from home, taking care of my basic needs and my kids' basic needs. It all makes a person seem incapable of simple tasks.

What I didn't even realize was that it had been a year since I'd worked with my life coach, and in that year, I'd made so much progress not just on my writing, but also on my self growth. I scrolled through my social media posts, realizing how much I'd accomplished. The whole reason I'd worked with a life coach was because I needed something just for me.

That day, I decided to shut the gate on those negative thoughts. I left them behind, because they weren't allowed in the new pasture I was creating. There was no way in hell I was going to give up on the one thing that I did for ME. It would not only be a disservice to myself, it would also be a disservice to my family and all of the others who were excited to read what I had to say.

I texted Josh while he was at work. I needed to vent about the day I was having, wallowing in the mess and my imposter syndrome.

"I am just going to buckle down and get these revisions done for my editor. I am going to keep the progress going on my children's book too." The text was immediately marked as read.

"Okay? Weren't you going to do that the whole time?" He always had a way of making me realize how hard I was on myself.

"Well, I don't know, I just feel like with everything that has happened, I might take a break," I texted back.

"Well I got your back, Kelc. I'm not sure when I have ever complained about the messy house either, it usually is only something that you talk about." Once again, he was right.

"I know, I just had to tell someone else. I am fine, I've got this." The text was read with no reply. He was at work, and I knew he probably had something going on.

I scanned our home one more time and realized that if I died tomorrow, no one would give a shit about my dirty house. My words, my stories, and my happiness—those would live on forever.

I shut the fucking gate on self-doubt, and that is when my writing journey really took off.

CHAPTER THIRTY

E

VEN WITH THE NOISE OF THE MUSIC, IT WAS SO QUIET OUT
in the pasture. All the fencing tools lay scattered, posts stacked
and ready to build the next fence. The sound of 94.3 KILO
streamed out of the maroon Chevy pickup. The vehicle was
parked with the doors wide open. Marilyn Manson sang his trou-
bled songs. I was too young to understand the lyrics and even his
eccentric getup, but I was in love with his music. It was him, and
The Offspring, and Ozzy Osbourne, Guns N' Roses, Linkin Park,
Rob Zombie…all of them had filled my ears with rock n' roll for
as long as I could remember.

It was almost as if we were in this bubble, and no other noise
in the world could get inside. It was just me, Dad, and the music.
No one could bother us, and that was my safe place. Like with
many other tasks on the ranch, I would watch. In and out, up
and down, the post hole diggers would work the Earth. We
would sing, and we would talk. Dad worked with such ease, but
now I realize it was all muscle memory. If you do something long
enough, it doesn't become easier; it just becomes second nature.

He'd lift a post off the pickup and set it in the hole. Sometimes he'd have to inspect it and twist it around to make sure it

would fit just right. I would come by with my shovel to make sure all the dirt got put back in the hole. I stomped my little cowpoke foot around the post to make sure the dirt was packed nice and tight, and damn did I feel important. The job usually finished with the wire stretchers and fencing pliers. *Pull, twist, bang! Pull, twist, bang!* He was so good at manipulating the wire. I had tried before, sometimes when he wasn't looking, but I could never do it with such swiftness. I handed him staples to secure the next wire. *Crack! Crack! Crack!* The pliers hit the staples. Over and over we did this. More rock music was sung, and more fence fixed.

The ranch wasn't always the Wild West that Western movies depicted. We weren't always hootin' and hollerin' or wrangling cattle. There were a lot of monotonous jobs, tasks that had to be done but weren't exactly exciting. Fixing fences with Dad actually happened to be one of my favorites. It was predictable, and it followed a pattern.

Each time we connected the wires to the fence post, filled the holes, and tightened the barbed wire, it was time to move on. The pickup would creep forward, and we would start all over. It was in those long hours doing the tedious work where I really found who I was as a kid.

While fixing fences, I embraced the calm. I packed my flower identification book with me. I studied the plants and the animals we saw along the way. The rhythmic sounds of the fencing tools and our favorite rock tunes made my mind feel so happy, free to think.

Most stories I tell of the ranch are filled with excitement and wonder, a country mouse version of Disneyland. Little do people know, it was within the mundane and the steady that I found my happiness. As I got older, I moved away from that way of thinking, only finding joy in the short bits of excitement when I *finished* something. Writing was continuous—the work was never really done, and even if it was, there was always a new story to tell.

On the ranch, there was always fence to fix.

———

April 2023

The familiar sound of the airline intercom called me and Mom onto our connecting flight. We had filled up at Starbucks and Chick-fil-A, both of us enjoying the time away from our mothering duties. Naturally, after having my epiphany about self-doubt, I found myself on another airplane.

This time I was on my way to Wisconsin, the land of cheese. It was a long way from the Wild West of Colorado, but I needed a new perspective. I'd found another woman on social media involved in agriculture who was hosting something called a mastermind. It was a place where women came together to talk about their goals. I saw that there was another children's author on the panel, and I wondered if I could gain insight and maybe a few fans among my Midwesterner friends.

Over the past month and a half, I'd done two passes through my manuscript, typing and tailoring until I was blue in the face. It was mundane, but I was happy. I was working toward a goal not to finish a book, but to find myself again within my writing. Since November, I'd completed three drafts, and the most current one was headed off to my professional editor for the very first time. My children's book was also being illustrated. As I worked with other professionals, I realized how far I had come and how proud I was that I didn't give up.

It seemed impossible, but once I got past my overwhelm and self-doubt, the boys were healthy, hearing, and wonderful again. Their surgeries were a success, and the recovery was finally 100 percent. They spent the days with me reading their favorite books, playing outside in the warming spring air, taking more walks, and being toddlers. They still weren't talking much, but I didn't even care anymore. They finally weren't at the mercy of their infected ears.

A storm rolled in as we flew to Lacrosse, Wisconsin. The airplane shook with aggression, turbulent enough to make a woman vomit. Seriously, she puked all over. We were traveling to a colder part of the country for only a single weekend. It wasn't the venue I needed, though—it was the perspective.

And perspective was exactly what I got. The women who spoke at the mastermind were all women blazing the trail to make their dreams come true. All of their dreams were very different, but they had one thing in common: all of them dealt with self-doubt as well. It was a fun feeling to be around other people who were self-sabotaged by their brains every once in a while, but found the strength in themselves to continue on.

My introverted tendencies were torn down by my excitement to talk with other women like me. I pushed myself to move around the room, participate in the activities, and really immerse myself in other women's thoughts. After being in my own head for the past few months, it was nice to be in someone else's. It was validating that when I told my story, these women wanted to hear more.

I spoke of my writing journey, and I realized that over recent months I was finding myself in the daily repetition of the keyboard. There was no one reading my writing; there was no book yet, no awards, and no certificates or degrees for the work I had done so far on my book. It was just becoming part of my day-to-day tasks, and although it wasn't glorious, it brought me comfort. I knew that the pages would be waiting for me every night when I put my kids to bed. I knew that with each story I wrote, I was finding my slow and steady and my predictable happiness again. I was proud of it too. I let everyone at the mastermind know that.

On our travels home, my brain hummed with ideas and contentment. I tried reading my book on the airplane and watching movies, but I couldn't help but write notes on my phone, creating more stories, more ideas filling my mind as the airplanes hopped home to warmer climates.

Our pastures on Rush Creek were large but divided by many fences. They built a framework for the ranch that kept the grass organized and the cattle healthy and safe. Each post hole dug, each wire stretched seemed very boring, but the structure as a whole was important. Although each chapter I wrote in my book seemed so tedious, it was part of a much larger message.

I was writing a book to heal myself. I was writing a book to encourage and relate to other women. Each step was important, and all of those tedious parts of my writing career had meaning. There wasn't a single paragraph that wasn't part of my personal growth.

My arrival home was a huge wake-up call. The mastermind had gears turning in my brain that I didn't even know existed. I was very focused on the books, the end products, but I knew being an author was much more than that.

Being an author was accepting each milestone as a success, even if it meant stepping away from the words to gain more perspective.

CHAPTER THIRTY-ONE

I HEAVED MYSELF UP, CATCHING MY KNEE IN THE STIRRUP. With another heave, my other leg swung over the saddle. The familiar squeaks and groans of the leather settled as I molded my skinny ass to the seat.

My posture corrected as I laid my reins to the left-hand side of my horse. I waited as Dad did the same. We were separating the mamas who'd had their babies from the ones who hadn't yet. This was a monotonous task, but again, one of my favorites. It took a lot of patience, and the baby calves needed slow movements. That was where I came in.

Dad sang cheerfully and looked at me for the next line of the *Sesame Street* song. I smirked, not playing along. I wasn't one who liked to be put on the spot.

He continued to belt the song as we rode away from the trailer. It was parked on the other side of the windmill that powered the tank below it.

The cattle started to swarm together as we pushed them around the tank. The action was natural for me, reining my horse, giving the mama cows their appropriate space. I'd become a hand. I wasn't a fast one, but I knew Dad needed me now. He told me so.

I was around twelve, and since we'd moved to Rush Creek, I'd become more and more helpful. Even though I always felt like more of a nuisance than an asset to the ranch, every year I was getting more knowledgeable. Was I slow? Absolutely, but my skills were definitely improving.

As we moved through the pasture, our small sprinkle of cattle grew like a snowball into a snowman; as we rolled farther across the grass, the ball got bigger. Soon the group became large enough that Dad patrolled both sides of the herd. I pushed the tail end, and we moved forward until we hit the fence line. It guided the mamas to their new home for calving season.

It was a normal experience to me that I was Dad's right-hand cowpoke. He had a few hired hands who came and went, but I was always there. When help was scarce, I was his only option. Although I know I frustrated him at times, he got used to being patient with the way I was. Even as I got older, when most kids started getting braver and faster, I was still slower than molasses. Beggars can't be choosers, right?

I pulled slightly on the reins, signaling my horse to ease up. The mamas needed space to find the gate. I looked across, watching Dad, moving in unison with him to get the girls in safely. The mamas and babies squished together. Their bodies shrunk through the gate. One row would move in, then we moved forward. The next row moved in, and we took another step with them.

There was something about moving cattle. It felt like a dance at times. The rhythm, the senses of all three animals, and the way they reacted to one another in unison was impressive. It was something I now realize I took for granted.

We were about to sort all of the mamas with babies away from the rest of the herd, and it was one of the more challenging aspects of my cowpoke career. "Kickin' off pairs," we liked to call it.

Pheweeeee!

The mamas moaned, and the babies called back. We waited, letting the pairs find each other. The move into the small corrals caused a little distress, and we needed them together to get the job done. Their calls all sounded the same to me, but within a few short minutes, each baby stuck to the side of their mama.

"You ready, girl?!" Dad shouted at me, making me flinch. I was focusing on the task ahead, and the human voice brought me out of the bellowing cow soundtrack.

I nodded.

We had to be certain that each mama had HER baby. The bond was important, both for us and for the cattle. No one was healthy without their mama.

"Let's go!" Dad headed into the herd and pointed to the first pair.

The maneuver was like the lift and peel of an orange. Dad was the starter—the fingernail, so to speak—picking out the pair. As he started the peel, I finished it, pulling the peel away from the rest of the fruit. One by one, we peeled the orange.

"Ride right at her, ride right at her!" Dad directed me as he peeled off each mama/baby pair. My slow pace, sometimes a hindrance, became a helpful vibe for the cattle. The mamas felt safe around me, and it made me proud that my skills were useful, and I could be myself.

Sorting pairs was something that took a lot of patience; it couldn't be rushed. The intricate details and the flow of cattle in and out of the herd took skill and practice. There were times we had to restart, and times when a squirrelly mama refused to be peeled off from the herd, but we always got the job done.

Others do these sorting challenges in an arena in front of crowds of people. Dad and I did it with a small audience: just God and His creations. The hard work that happens behind the scenes of a cattle operation is often not appreciated. There's much more to the Western world than riding bulls and team roping in arenas.

Becoming an author was very similar. There was no instant gratification. It was a system of turning gears, and without one, the system failed. I learned to slow down. A book could only be written one word at a time. It was much more than the glossy images I'd envisioned when I started. I saw shiny lights and book signings, but I didn't have a clue about the amount of work that went into it.

Every detail and step mattered, regardless of how small it was. A five hundred-word sprint could mean just as much as the two thousand-word edit you did the day before. You might erase half of your book and start all over, and your readers would never know. It's one of the most mentally tasking challenges I have ever attempted, including sorting skittish mama cows with their running babies.

After my trip to Wisconsin in April, I was waiting for professionals to do their work. My memoir was being edited for the first time, and my children's book was finishing up its illustrations. I took this time to reflect on everything that had happened in the past year of this journey. The culmination of events hit me all at once, and I couldn't help but sit with gratitude. My patience was paying off, and all of the little details I was handling in my own business were becoming part of who I was. When you do something for so long, it can start to feel mundane, but that monotony becomes skill. The slow-moving process becomes second nature.

Once again, I'd found myself in my childhood. I just exchanged my saddle for my keyboard.

CHAPTER THIRTY-TWO

I DUG MY LITTLE FINGER IN THE SAND, FIRST TRACING A K, then a diamond. I added a dot in the middle of the shape to add a little flare. We sat next to the propane tank across from the ranch house, taking a break from our work. The ground was cool where we sat, and I was fixated on the drawings in the sand.

"The K will blotch; it isn't a good letter to brand with," Dad explained as he drew a quarter circle in the sand next to mine. One of our hobbies was creating cattle brands that we liked. He used to explain to me how a single-iron brand was very cool and efficient. We compared which letters tended to look better on the hips of animals other cowboys had. They were unique to the ranches that owned them, identifying each animal legally. The brands represented the way of life that the cowboys had chosen. It was a symbol of our traditions that lived on from one generation to the next.

We continued to draw ideas, one after the other. The killdeer birds landed and grasshoppers stuck to the legs of my jeans. I knew it wasn't long before we would need to go saddle our horses. Dad waited for me to finish my peanut butter sandwich, but his comment about my brand idea annoyed me. I was only five years old, but I knew that a brand represented ownership.

"I don't care if it blotches, I want it to have a K in it," I argued with Dad as he got up off of the ground. "K, diamond, dot. That will be my brand, OK Dad?" I made sure he knew I was still going to do it regardless of his advice.

"OK," he said as he opened the gates to the corrals. "You don't want to work with me, though!" He shook his head as we walked down the alley to the barn.

"I'm going to! And also, I'm going to be a bull rider, OK Dad?" I continued to make sure he knew I was ignoring his input. He didn't really have a choice whether to agree with me or not.

I waited in the doorway of the barn as he grained the horses and draped a halter over 202's neck. When he tied up my ride for the day, I dragged the curry comb over my sorrel gelding's hair. The reddish brown became shinier with each stroke, the comb breaking away the particles of dirt.

I was alone in the barn, still dwelling on my brand. While some little girls were dreaming of barrel racing or being the county fair queen, I was dreaming of owning my own cattle.

May 2023

The illustrations for my children's book landed in my inbox. A cartoon version of the little cowpoke I was on the ranch stared back at me. The Big Magic that had visited me a few months ago had come to life on the pages. The pride and nostalgia I felt looking at the front cover overwhelmed me, and I knew this was the positive fun I needed to get through my memoir revisions.

I laughed to myself when I read the lines...

"It wasn't a simple one, two, three."

"There was failure and practice, patience is key."

The book was about swinging ropes and riding horses, but it was a funny reminder to myself that becoming an author isn't just a simple one, two, three.

The past couple of months, I had been writing words *and* building a business. When you self-publish a book, you become the marketing team, the PR team, the funding, the boss, and the employee.

I would be lying if I said I hadn't lost my shit multiple times during this whole process. The revisions to my memoir were really starting to make me crazy. I had read the pages and revisited the same stories so many times that I started to feel the fatigue.

Seeing the illustrations for my picture book really helped break up this tasking journey, but it also brought up the realization that I would soon have to upload the files, get the copyright pages completed, and upload them to two different printing companies.

With the children's book almost complete, I released it to my fans for preorder. My phone dinged—email after email with notifications of another book sale. With each ding, I found myself a little bit more stressed, knowing I was going to have to package and send all of these books that were selling. I was happy, but just a smidge overwhelmed.

The next day, I got another notification that threw me off. This time, it was a Facebook message from a name I didn't recognize.

"Hey Kelcie, we were wondering if you could do an interview for our paper." The *Kiowa County Independent* was contacting me to do an article about my author journey. It was the county I showed goats in, the county where I attended the gymkhana and tried out for Tiny Tot Princess. The newspaper in the county I grew up next to on Rush Creek wanted *me* to do an interview for them.

For a year, I had been building this business and fighting off self-doubt. It was very uncomfortable for me to write for other people, let alone market myself as my personal brand. I was posting to multiple social media platforms, writing for my audience, and communicating more than I was ever used to. If I wanted others to believe in me, I had to believe in myself. It's a struggle I still face every day as an author. Receiving that notification was a huge validation that all of the hours spent writing and creating content was worth it.

Obviously I agreed to answer some questions for the newspaper, but when I sent my email in, they had yet another surprise for me. Not only did they want an interview, they also wanted me to write for their lifestyle column once a month.

After all the times I had wanted to give up, this had happened because I didn't. The birth of my boys and becoming a mother in such extreme circumstances changed me as a person. It began as a journey to find myself again, but I soon realized it wasn't that at all. I had to figure out who the *new* me was going to be. I was completely rebranding myself as a woman, a mother, and now an author. The old me was morphing into someone new, and I used writing as a way to figure that out.

As I emailed the woman from the newspaper back, I once again felt overwhelmed by all of the emotions this journey brought on. So many aspects of my life were coming full circle, including interviewing for the newspaper that was located where all my stories began.

It turns out I wasn't going to own my own cattle brand. I was going to *be* my own brand. My books would be my cattle, and maybe my name would be recognized all over the world. Granted, this was just a local newspaper, but how much farther could I go if I never gave up?

CHAPTER THIRTY-THREE

When the door on the freestanding stove closed, fumes of ether filled the air. The body of the apparatus was a fifty-gallon metal drum piped out the top of the shop, a source of heat in the winter. Beers cracked and conversation continued as Dad found me a soda in the medicine fridge.

The cold months had arrived.

When Dad's work with the cattle slowed to daily checks and breaking ice, we occupied a lot of our time tinkering in the shop. I learned to reload bullets, following the assembly line of steps. There was empty brass, gunpowder, and primers along with the bullet itself. These weapons were usually used to eradicate pests from the ranch, and reloading each shell was a reminder of how lethal the small objects were when loaded into the chamber.

Dad cleared large areas of the concrete for me to ride my scooter round and round, circle after circle. My tire tracks permanently streaked the floor.

Levi, our day worker, friend, and, after a while, my non-blood uncle, was there with us that evening. We posted our chairs around the stove, cozy next to its warmth. The second beer cracked and I knew it was going to be a good night. I heard the same stories several times over, but they still made me laugh. On the off chance you heard some small town drama, it was understood that information never left the shop. The conversations were easy, and there weren't really any valuable lessons within their back-and-forth. But the constant movement of words without breaks in between signified a long-lasting friendship.

I was a quiet kid, and I sat and listened intently, enjoying my soda alongside the cowboys' beers. As Dad threw back more beers, I always took the opportunity to con him into doing my chores the next morning. He always kept his word too; I never got yelled at when I slept in on those days. I spit on the stove, mimicking the two men beside me. The saliva sizzled on the hot metal, and it was so satisfying, I understood why they did it so often.

The nights were warm with fire and a sense of togetherness. Most ten-year-olds probably didn't enjoy this type of company, but I did. The friendship the cowboys exhibited was endearing, and it was a different side of them. I often saw them wrangling cattle and sweating through their hats. It was a nice change to hear them let loose and relax a little.

Levi was family, and it made sense why. When you're working in the middle of nowhere, in the elements, and from time to time in dicey situations, God gives you no choice but to become friends. Doing hard things together creates loyalty, and the ranch made it easy to weed out who was loyal and who wasn't.

Becoming an author brought so many unexpected changes in my life, including in my friend groups. Having my kids was a big eye-opener to who was in my village, and writing a book changed the dynamic of that village tremendously. There were strangers more invested in my story than people I thought were close to me. I noticed I hadn't seen friends who I used to hang out with, and our lives seemed to drift apart. In some ways, I felt sad. It was like I was saying goodbye to a period of my life. In other ways, I was excited to get to know these new people who were so invested in me.

I was finally done trying to get approval from *everyone.* I found myself appreciating those people who stuck with me through my postpartum journey, and the ones who cheered me on when I first started writing, rather than when I started getting recognized. They were the ones offering to help with my kids, shooting me positive texts, letting me have a good cry every once in a while. Those same people who were with me in my darkest times deserved to see me step into the light of my motherhood and author journey. They were my Levis. They were the ones who were there when we were up to our ears in cattle, the ones who would ride along with you in the raging heat and break ice in the blistering cold. They were there during the droughts and the rainy seasons.

When you start becoming successful by your own standards, those who aren't on the same level want nothing to do with you. Some are unwilling to take the leap with you. Don't be angry with them; they're happy where they're at, and that is OK. I liked the person I was becoming, and I only wanted people around me who liked her too. The author I was becoming was full of creativity and spontaneity. I put myself out there, and I wasn't afraid of what people thought of me anymore. I was relieved when I realized I wasn't responsible for the way people saw me. I was only responsible for the way I saw myself.

I decided that I could waste my time being upset about fading relationships, or I could move forward and cherish the friends that I had. I kept writing, and I kept updating my fans. I kept posting on my social media, and I continued to push away self-doubt. I continued to let people phase out of my life. It wasn't a bad breakup, just a necessary absence—acquaintances rather than besties.

I deserved happiness, and the real friends I was finding deserved to be the ones beside me drinking beers and shooting the shit when the hard times let up. I couldn't have done any of this without them.

CHAPTER THIRTY-FOUR

THE TREES HUMMED IN UNISON, LOCUSTS COVERING EVERY inch they could find to play their harmonic songs. I sifted through the trees, mason jar in hand, plucking them from their positions in the orchestra. They had become one of our favorite baits for catfish, and the grandparents were headed out to the ranch to go fishing.

Coolers were packed with hot dogs and lunch meat. Tackle boxes and sleeping bags filled the beds of our trucks, and we were off to the catfish dam. The two-tracks led us through the pastures on the west side of Rush Creek, and I was eager to feel the first tug on my line.

When we pulled up to the dam, cattle scattered through the mud. They were basking in the sun, flies swarming around them. The horizon was transitioning from yellow to orange, welcoming the sun to the other hemisphere. It was times like these that I really did think God was with me. No person could ever make something so beautiful and peaceful.

Dad prepared the bonfire, throwing old fence posts into a pile for later. Coolers scraped the back of the pickup as we pulled them off to prepare food for the evening. I found the jar of locusts I'd collected earlier, and I knew I was going to have a good fishing day.

I had learned to cast a fishing pole long before most, and I threw my line with my freshly picked cicada with an ease that was quite impressive for a seven-year-old. Cast after cast I threw, munching on dill pickle potato chips. I didn't have a care in the world that there was dam water on my fingers from unhooking my little catches of the day. I was in my element.

The air started to cool, and I felt my stomach start to rumble. The chips weren't going to hold me over much longer. I walked back to the pickup, searching for the cookies Grammy had brought with her. I was careful walking through the hardened mud. The imprints the cattle left with their feet made great ankle-breakers.

I shoved cookies in my mouth and decided to cast one more time before I went and roasted some weenies and s'mores on the fire. When I cast the line, the locust flew, pulling my line even farther across the dam. The shimmering water splashed when my bait hit the surface. I anxiously anticipated the sudden jolt a fish would make on the line. The sensation that followed wasn't a familiar bite, but it was still a bite.

My line tugged slightly, and I pulled, ready to reel in a small fish. The goal was to never get skunked. Going the entire night without catching a fish was a real letdown, and no matter what age you were, the shit-talking wasn't off limits.

Except this time, the drag on the line seemed heavier—no fighting like catches I'd made before. I continued to reel, worried I had caught a big piece of moss. Another tug on the line confirmed a fish was still there.

"I think I got a big one guys." I looked to each side of me as I reeled the line in.

"Do you need help?!" Grammy yelled from her fishing position.

"No I got it, I got it!" There was no way in hell I was letting anyone take any credit for this one. This was going to be the fishing story of a lifetime.

The fight continued, and I saw a piece of fish surface. My eyes widened in excitement. I feared I would lose the monster! As soon as he hit the muddy dirt, I ran forward, making sure I had him close. He was the biggest fish I had seen come out of one of our dams, and I had caught him!

Dad ran forward, grabbing the fish before it could get away from me. My smile took up my entire face, which wasn't hard to do with my massive teeth coming in after first grade.

He was eleven pounds, so large I rode him like a horse in the photo to show proof. Grammy watched me, jealous, but happy for her granddaughter who'd just caught the big one. I baited the hook, I got in the mud, and I caught the fish all on my own.

Papa took the massive fish, fileting it with his electric knife. The gray skin peeled back from the meat, exposing the chicken-like flesh. The fish I'd just caught was going to feed us later when we traveled home. From catching the locusts to throwing the fish nuggets on ice, it was a rewarding process. I had eaten fish at the store, and ordered it at restaurants, but it was pretty cool to be involved in every part of the journey.

The night was spent around the fire. I ate s'mores in celebration and listened to ghost stories. The sky was full of stars, and I wondered how much better life could get. I listened intently as Dad relived the moment he saw a ghost in our old ranch home. The seriousness on his face made it even spookier. The prairie sprawled out behind me, and I felt myself looking over my shoulder, not trusting what else could be lurking in the night.

I fell asleep in the front seat of our pickup, and when I woke, the morning sun was already heating up the cab. Sweat soaked my back. I looked out the window, watching my parents and grandparents prepare the area to leave. My sister was already awake eating snacks, sitting in the only chair that hadn't been picked up yet.

The ride home wasn't as exciting as the ride there, but I knew my fish was in the cooler waiting to be breaded and fried. I eagerly helped everyone put away the fishing poles, unload the coolers, and throw away the trash we'd collected during our overnight stay. My grandparents, still jealous of my giant catch, gave me another congratulatory hug before leaving for home.

I packed my Ziplock of raw fish home. Dad helped me batter the nuggets. The deep fryer sizzled as we dropped the catch into the hot oil. I admired all the hard work I had done to bring our dinner home. It made the fried catfish taste that much better. The crunch was perfect, and as we ate, I felt warm with happiness. Our time together and the journey to the dinner table was so much fun. It was something most kids didn't get to experience like I did.

With many things in life, we as humans try to rush through the process to get to the end. Fishing, and many other experiences I had growing up, were full of step-by-step processes. With no bait, there were no fish. There were learning curves, strategies, and so many lessons learned while living in God's Country. Only as a child, I never focused on the outcome of each process. I trusted them. I had fun with them.

I started by saddling my horse, taking the first step into the water, catching the cicadas, and backing up a trailer… Each wild story started somewhere, and it ended either in great triumph or great failure. Regardless, I was so brave, and I appreciated the journey each day brought on Rush Creek.

My childhood was spent cowpokin' and discovering nature. Each day and each task was part of a much bigger picture. I either enjoyed those small moments, or I learned from the struggles that came along the way. It was a much simpler time, and it's hard to say why we lose that as adults. We all tend to lose ourselves at some point, and a great majority of us never find who we want to be until it's too late.

When I had my kids, I had to work through a lot of issues to get me where I am today. My beginning in motherhood was not what I expected. Let me rephrase that: I was BLINDSIDED. Motherhood was like finding a needle in a haystack—a really large haystack that also happened to be on fire. Many times, I had a victim attitude, and I felt like the world was out to get me. The reflections of the ranch, where nature takes its course, reminded me just how wrong I was. The world doesn't care about you and your problems. Only you do.

I pulled up emotions each night when I hit the keyboard, and there were times it left me exhausted. Experiencing my life through words on paper, and growing as a person because of it, was uncomfortable yet rewarding. The weight of guilt and self-doubt lifted with each chapter I wrote. My confidence as an author grew with each milestone I accomplished in the writing process.

My keyboard is worn. My soul is healed. My heart is full. This book comes to a close, and I can't help but wonder: What if all women could do this? What if we could all have the courage to travel back to the deep moments in our lives and grow from them? What if we could acknowledge the hardships and cry? What if we could look back at all the special moments and remember to create more?

As I close this final chapter, I wonder.

Maybe we're all just cowpokes who cry?

ABOUT THE AUTHOR

Kelcie Martin is a former cowpoke from eastern Colorado. She grew up on a forty thousand acre cattle ranch, and decided it was time to share her stories with the world! She lives in southern Colorado with her husband and twin boys. They all keep her busy while she works from home as a high school science teacher. You can find her on TikTok, Instagram, and Facebook @cowpokeswhocry.